JESUS, RELIGION

SPIRITUALITY

Phillippa Leslie

A CHALLENGING OBSERVATION
OF ESTABLISHED RELIGIONS AND ALTERNATIVE
BELIEFS

ISBN-13: 978-1546626367

ISBN-10: 1546626360

Published 2017

Hawkmedia.co.uk

JESUS, RELIGION & SPIRITUALITY

This book is merely a layman's view of the many religions and beliefs, both past and present, that have formed the basis of people's lives. It is not a historical account of bygone events, but is a step back from, and a contemporary look at, the beliefs and practices that we have grown up with, both current and extinct, plus some that may not be quite so familiar. This is an appraisal of how humans through the ages have dealt with heart break, joy, pain and celebration in the form of worship; the other side of the coin being an infiltration of a darker force, practiced usually in secret, and generally to be feared.

I have given here my thoughts with regard to the life of Jesus; who he really was; whether the Bible stories about his life are to be taken at face value; are the many translations and interpretations providing us with an accurate and unbiased view? Many of us believe in a higher power of some description, be it an idol, prophet, spirit, or some other form of significance, and I have attempted to explore just some of them that most of us are aware of.

My own ancestors were missionaries in India in the early 1800's, suffering severe hardship, but facing it all with courage and tenacity. Hopefully they will forgive this rather broad appraisal of a subject that has not only fascinated, but also transformed, many of us throughout our lives.

Phillippa Leslie

DEDICATION

To both my mother and my father, whose considerable literary and artistic talents went largely unrecognized. Without them my inheritance may well have been bleak, and this book never written.

To my 'missionary' ancestors who showed tremendous courage and tenacity in those early days, bringing Christianity to remote regions of India. Hopefully, in the great beyond, they will have mellowed with time and will forgive, and perhaps not condemn too harshly, my indulgence in an alternative understanding of 'belief' in this turbulent world of ours.

Although my attitude towards 'religion' has altered over the years, I am however, a deeply spiritual person, and hope the views I now portray will be of interest.

For Seekers of the Truth

The views expressed in this publication are those of the author's. The information and the interpretation of that information are presented in good faith. Readers are advised that where controversial issues are involved, they have a personal responsibility for making their own assessments and their own ethical judgement

Contents

FOOD FOR THOUGHT

We are, as a species, curious. If it were not for our ingenuity and curiosity we would not have evolved into the super-brains we are today. Why then has it taken us so long to question the Bible and the parables portrayed in it?

Most of my life I have believed in 'religion', having been brought up in a Church of England family, my mother having been, what I thought to be, quietly religious. My father had no belief that he actively showed to any of us. With hindsight I am now wondering if her thoughts were more along the lines of my own – non church-going and spiritual, as opposed to 'religious'. Somehow our beliefs have become distorted, our own misguided interpretations woven into the original message, some religions becoming so disturbed as to be criminal.

Jesus was a man of principle, and ultimately 'love', forgiving disloyalty and acts of violence even before they occurred. Looking at it all from a logical point of view, and one that perhaps others might agree with, I have attempted to put my thoughts on paper.

My fascination with Jesus and the various aspects of religion came about in earnest when I discovered a book by the theologian Dr. Barbara Thiering, doctor of Divinity and researcher of the Dead Sea Scrolls. Her interpretation of biblical events seemed perfectly feasible and altogether logical, and the more I thought about it the more convinced I became.

According to her research, Jesus was born an Essene. His parents, Mary and Joseph, were both Essenes. That is to say they belonged to a religious order who believed, amongst other things, that sex was not to be practised unless for the procreation of children, celibacy being the highest way of life. There were very strict rules where marriage was concerned, affording long periods of time (and celibacy) between betrothal (engagement) and actual consummation of a marriage that took place after an interval of three years from the time of that engagement.

Joseph being the heir to the David throne, it was of vital importance to the Essenes that the royal line of David should continue. They were members of the Zadoks and the Davids, having been high priests and kings of Israel before the destruction of the temple in the 6th century BC. The line was therefore continued with the birth of Jesus. However, during the three year 'betrothal' period of Joseph and Mary's forthcoming marriage, instead of keeping apart from each other, Jesus was conceived. As the Essenes intended to restore a David king, the question of whether Jesus was legitimately conceived was a crucial one. From a strictly conventional point of view he was an illegitimate child of Joseph, and could not inherit. Their name for Jesus was 'The Man of a Lie' referring both to his teachings and to his illegitimacy. Some saw him as of no consequence, whereas to others he was a King-Messiah, who was potentially even higher in exaltation than a king. When his brother James was born into a legitimate marriage, there were those who believed *he* was the true heir to the throne. Jesus was affected all his life by this confusion, and stain on his legitimacy.

If we are to believe the circumstances of Jesus' birth according to the Bible, it reads as almost a 'fairytale'. The words Virgin, Angel etc. have altered so much in meaning over time as to be meaningless. A 'virgin' in those times referred to Vestal virgins, the word virgin meaning a kind of nun. Mary was a virgin, meaning nun, betrothed to Joseph. The word virgin alone has instilled in us the mystically divine parable that is our acceptance of Jesus' birth today. When Mary the virgin conceived, which was unfortunately within the designated period of abstinence, Joseph was then in a very tenuous position. He had committed an offence according to the rules of the Essenes, and on being uncertain as to what to do, he sought advice from an 'angel'. It was believed that priests and levites were considered to be heavenly beings – 'gods' and 'angels', and seem always to have been men. *Could it possibly be that the elaborate story of the birth of Jesus having occurred through 'divine intervention' was just an ingeniously elaborate verbal concoction, invented by those in power, to cover up the fact that the heir to the David throne would in fact be regarded as illegitimate? This highly embarrassing faux pas, and political and hereditary disaster, had to be explained in a way that the people could accept and revere (the populous at that time being extremely superstitious and gullible), therefore legitimising the birth of the heir. This fictional narrative would quite conceivably have been embellished over time to captivate an attentive audience, culminating in the story of the birth that we know today.*

To quote Dr. Barbara Thiering:-

"When Jesus was 'tempted by Satan', he was in fact having political discussions with Judas Iscariot, called 'Satan' as a leader of political revolutionaries. When Jesus 'ascended into heaven', he actually went to a monastery, called 'heaven' because it was the place where priests and levites, called 'gods' and 'angels', conducted a perpetual liturgy.

When 'a star guided the wise men' to the birthplace of Jesus, there was no real star. It was Joseph, his father, who was the Star of David, leading the Magians, his political associates, to witness the fact that an heir to his dynasty had been born.

The 'raising of Lazarus' was a lifting of the excommunication of an expelled monk, who had 'died', because excommunication was treated as a spiritual death".

When Jesus began his preaching he must have been an extremely charismatic figure with a commanding presence for so many to have become enraptured enough to follow him, facing possible death in their beliefs. To outward appearances he would have seemed a rather enigmatic figure, though being a carpenter's son he would, I imagine, have been quite strong. He was also a gentle man with infinite compassion, wisdom, and understanding of others, though when occasion arose was not averse to bouts of anger. Women, I'm sure, must have loved him, seeing in him a quality no other man could possibly aspire to, and the men would have sought his approval for the same reason. His teachings appear to have been of a spiritual nature, not 'religious' in the sense of the word, and as 'radical' as he could have been within the confines of the culture at that time – those confines proving, in the end, to be his undoing. He was above religion, and in present-day terms, was trying to lift people into a higher realm, 'the bigger picture', not adhering to any particular doctrine. He appears to have been a healer performing, what would seem to be, 'miracles'. We have our healers today, who also perform life changing miracles, with certainty that their power comes from God, a higher power, or universal 'energy', the strength of which cannot be refuted. We are beings of spirit energy and light, and through channelling our thoughts onto a higher plain, and tapping into that energy, we can reach a higher state of consciousness and understanding.

I am of the opinion that Jesus *lived*, and in my own mind there is little doubt. The fact that his name is on our lips two thousand years hence would seem to render his authenticity beyond question, along with other notable figures in our history books. Whether he died on the cross is up for conjecture. I believe that, after having been laid in the tomb (a cave), he was administered to (possibly by his brother James, or Joseph of Arimathea as he was sometimes known, who owned the garden of Gethsemane and the tomb within it) with certain healing properties which eventually brought him round, and it would appear, he 'rose from the dead'. Jesus would have had to have left the Holy Land for his own safety, and I believe he went on to live a normal life, reaching into his seventies, possibly coming to this country at some time; I refer to William Blake's hymn "And did those feet in ancient times walk upon England's mountains green? And was the Holy Lamb of God on England's pleasant pastures seen?" Legend has it that he travelled to Kashmir in India and is buried in a tomb in the city of Srinagar. Other accounts of his life have been recorded where he settled with Mary Magdalene in France, then known as Gaul, in the town of Rennes-le-Chateau, ultimately dying there.

Mary Magdalene was Jesus' wife, and bore him first a daughter, Sarah, and then two sons, the eldest also called Jesus, who would inherit the royal title of David on his father's death. I am inclined to think that perhaps the title of 'prostitute' came about through possible jealousy of Mary's exalted state in the eyes of Jesus (or perhaps, dare I say, a mis-translation in the Bible?). In the painting of 'The Last Supper' by Leonardo da Vinci, which covers the end wall of the refectory of the Dominican convent of Santa Maria delle Grazie in Milan, seated on the right hand of Jesus is a figure that only now has actually been thoroughly scrutinized. The figure would seem to be that of John but on closer inspection is definitely a female, with feminine features, long hair and with her hands entwined in front of her, Mary Magdalene. She is seen seated on Jesus' right side with her head almost resting on the shoulder of one of the apostles. If we juxtapose the positions of Jesus and Mary, with her body on his left, we see that she fits perfectly against that of his. Long before any of us dared to question, did Leonardo discover the 'truth', and this tantalizing work go unchallenged until now? In recent years this particular painting has become synonymous with spiritual symbolism and fascinating speculation and enigma, inspiring both authors and film producers in a *search for the truth*.

Richard Atwood, in his work *'Mary Magdalene in the New Testament Gospels and Early Tradition'*, explores the possibility that Mary Magdalene, far from being of lowly birth, was in actual fact from a royal background. Her mother's name was Eucharia and her father's name was Syro; they came from Syria. Through inheritance from their mother, she and her sister Martha came into possession of three properties, the Castle Magdalene, Bethany and part of Jerusalem. The possibility that Mary was a wealthy woman would have secured her independence and enabled her to provide financial support for Jesus' cause.

Perhaps we can now separate the truth from wishful thinking and look more deeply at the substance of the man himself. Some of us would like to believe that Jesus was divine, a 'heavenly being', and not of our earthly existence. However, I believe him to have been a mortal being with the greatest compassion and feeling for mankind. He was certainly a specially gifted person, unusually sensitive and in tune with the sick, the poor, and those in need of comfort. Undoubtedly he was a courageous emissary, and one of the most exceptional figures in our western history, carrying a life saving message, and willing to die for us in the belief that he was right. We know he was right. We all seem to have lost our way, and this chaotic world seems to have forgotten how powerful that message was, conveyed so long ago. Going to church will not save us, but getting closer to a 'spiritual' understanding might. There are those who feel they have been chosen as 'messengers of God', but all too often do not get the message right.

Through the ages 'holy' men have invented different rituals to be performed during services etc., basically I suspect, to make them feel and appear more pious, bringing about a false sense of righteousness. The 'higher' the church the more these rituals are practiced, Christianity actually having been hijacked by the Church. A priesthood was constructed, the truth becoming obscured and knowledge of the original message lost. Instead of being a vehicle for truth, the Church has become a vehicle for power and repression.

Any evidence that contravenes the biblical accounts of 'creation' etc. have been kept well and truly under wraps, and it is only recently that historians and archaeologists have had the courage to speak out and present us with proof. This contradictory evidence undermines the very foundations on which the 'Christian' Church is built, and the enforced belief adhered to by millions of steadfast 'churchgoers', the majority of these churchgoers believing that enlightenment will be their reward for devout adherence to the traditional acceptance of the Scriptures.

How many innocent souls have died in the name of 'religion'? How can people follow a religion that is based on violence? How can people frequent places of worship and immediately after prayer commit despicable crimes against humanity? This is not 'religion' of a divine or inspirational nature, but an excuse for venting anger against an opposing group of people who differ in opinion. The majority do not take the time to think whether it is right or wrong but follow blindly. Most religions stem from a force for good, but some have become a force for evil. The somewhat revered word 'religion' does not seem to apply to the world in which we now live and are familiar with, this being one of violence in its name. It is more like gang warfare, with nothing remotely 'holy' about it.

How can there be a 'holy war' when Jesus' teachings were always against any form of violence? Why is it that people think their going to church every Sunday automatically makes them good, or at the very least accepted, supposedly establishing a Godly position in life? I believe that those who base their lives on religion are using it rather as a security blanket, a safeguard against their possible entry into 'hell'. Also to live your life constantly in the reassuring knowledge that you are never alone seems to be essential to our individual stability. Perhaps it would be possible for everyone to take a step back and look at it all from a distance? Ask yourself *"why"?*

Spirituality becomes a way of life for those who look beyond the traditional and who have reached a higher level of thinking and understanding. To have various different religions, individually believing they are the 'one true light' is not feasible. We are all spiritual beings and do not *require* religious doctrine to be accepted as 'good' people. In words we have heard before - *"The Kingdom of God is within you, not in buildings of wood and stone".*

All nature that we see around us, and all that exists beyond, resonates to the beat of a primordial drum. We did not *invent* spirituality, it has always been the basis of our psyche since time immemorial. Man has always sought to improve his lot and the world around him by appealing to, what he considers to be, a being of higher denomination, albeit idols or spirits, believing that in them lies a higher power which can come to his assistance if 'prayed' to diligently. We have always *felt* the resonance of life around us, but have not always interpreted its actuality correctly, thinking that we could manipulate it to suit our own ends. Therein lies the *'power of positive thinking'* which, by harnessing and focusing the energy around us, can very often produce spectacular results. However, we do not always get what we wish for, and our own unique life in this universe travels along its own designated path regardless.

EARTH'S ENERGY

The body's energy system plays an extremely important role in the maintenance of our health, and our very lives. However, this has been largely ignored in the Western world of medical science. All of us, at one time or another, have felt 'lack of energy' or 'extremely tense', according to the flow of energy through our bodies. All organs and systems in our bodies are interrelated, and are all interdependent. The energies which allow us to breathe, move and talk, and which allow all our organs and senses to function, are the same as those which allow all nature around us to function; fire to burn, rocks to form, trees and seeds to grow, rain to fall, and the wind to blow.

Over five thousand years' ago in the Far East medical practitioners began to explore theories relating our energies to the energies in the surrounding universe. They eventually devised a system of five basic elements, which were identified as Earth, Gold, Water, Wood and Fire. They then, in turn, related each of these elements to each of our major organs. Thus, 'earth' describes the energy of the stomach and spleen, 'gold' the lungs and respiratory system, 'water' the kidneys and urinary system, 'wood' the liver, and 'fire' the energy of the heart, these five elements reflecting closely the characteristics of that particular organ. Through this system, we can work with our elements to bring more balance to our physical, mental and emotional bodies.

Each of us emits unique energy patterns. Although it may be faint, the energy from every individual, who has lived on this planet, is still radiating through the universe. The earth moves around the sun, the sun around the milky way, and our galaxy through the universe. We are collecting information from the universe every instant. We are one with our world, our own energies interacting with each other and the universe, and are continually emitting energy into our surroundings.

The energy field that surrounds us is called the 'Aura'. The Chinese call it 'Chi', the Indians 'Prana', and in Christian teachings it is 'Light'. The aura is made up of multiple layers of energy that vibrate at different frequencies, each layer having its own particular function. There are seven layers, all fusing with each other, connecting to a certain 'chakra' on the body, all working together. These layers have to maintain a balance with the chakras for us to experience good health. We are all subtly interconnected to all other matter in the observable universe because we are universal creatures. This is the 'enlightenment' that mystics and great scientists like Albert Einstein realised:-

"A human being is part of the whole, called by us "universe", a part limited in time and space. We experience ourselves, our thoughts and feelings, as something separate from the rest; a kind of optical delusion of consciousness. This delusion is a kind of prison for us, restricting us to our personal desires and to affection for a few persons nearest to us. Our task must be to free ourselves from the prison by widening our circle of compassion, to embrace all living creatures and the whole of nature in its beauty......The true value of a human being is determined primarily by the measure and the sense in which they have obtained liberation from the self......We shall require a substantially new manner of thinking if humanity is to survive".

"I fear the day that technology will surpass our human interaction. The world will have a generation of idiots". Albert Einstein

"I firmly believe that before many centuries more, Science will be the master of man. The engines he will have invented will be beyond his strength to control. Someday science itself shall have the existence of mankind in its power and the human race

commit suicide by blowing up the world." Henry Adams, 11th April, 1862.

The above was written by the philosopher Henry Adams, grandson of American President John Quincy Adams, and whose life was rooted in American political aristocracy that emerged from the American Revolution.

FOOD FOR THOUGHT (Cont'd)

Praying to idols and spirits creates a false sense of security, and as we are fully aware, any amount of praying will not stop global catastrophes from occurring or exclude our sons and daughters from dying amidst the horrors of war. When these disasters do occur, it seems that believers in a loving God are willing to believe that it is 'God's will' and that there must be some meaningful plan behind it. I find this quite disturbing, as what could a loving God possibly have in mind which would exonerate wreaking such devastation and heartbreak on innocent people?

There are those who believe that acts of violence committed under the auspices of 'religion' relinquishes them from any blame. When we go to war, as in the past, we pray that God will be on our side, protecting us from harm, and that we shall experience a resounding victory over our enemies. However, *all* participants are praying the same thing! If God heard and answered everyone's prayers we should all be winners without doubt!

I find it hard to accept that a Priest or Vicar, the Pope or Archbishop for that matter, is really any more righteous than a fellow human being who lives a caring and compassionate spiritual existence. Surely a messenger of 'God', spreading the teachings of Jesus, should emulate his humble lifestyle and encourage us to do the same, basing our lives on the less 'material'. To assume that Jesus would be impressed by the ornate gold trimmings that embellish our churches, or the money that pours in from unsuspecting parishioners to bolster the church fund, would be the antithesis of all that he believed in. For the clergy to raise themselves to such untouchably 'divine' heights I find rather insulting to my own intelligence and belief. This exalted position is not bestowed by 'God' but by man, and is far more grandiose than that of Jesus himself. A Roman Catholic priest for instance, although he would profess to be a messenger of a 'loving' God, has the power to completely terrify a troubled sinner into thinking he will be 'damned' and go to hell should he not repent, saying several 'Hail Mary's' in abject contrition until it is considered he is sufficiently chastened. This is a religion based on *fear*, fear of being damned and of going to Hell. The subject in question will probably then go on to do exactly the same thing again, feeling free to do so as long as he confesses his sins to a priest, that priest having bestowed upon himself the power to 'forgive' in the name of God. Catholicism allowed sinners to be fully absolved and re-qualify for admission into Paradise. This guarantee of absolution at any time, regardless of the degree of sin, proved enormously popular, a simple step towards the eradication of guilt. It also put the Catholic Church in the incredibly powerful position of knowing who was doing what and to whom, allowing for what might be seen to be the most successful example of moral blackmail of all time! For a Catholic priest to lead a life of complete and utter celibacy goes against our biological make-up, and as we have seen in the past (and indeed this is happening at this very moment) some priests have found this to be impossible, leading outwardly 'God-fearing' lives while at the same time behaving despicably, and often criminally. How can this religion hold its head up high and profess to act in the name of 'God' when attempting to cover up and exonerate the sickening actions of some of its members - a very hypocritical 'religion'; also, insisting that the children from a union between a Catholic and a non-Catholic should *automatically* be seen to be Catholic is a very clever ploy to swell numbers and increase their already immense power!

Over the centuries the followers of the teachings of Jesus have turned what he would have termed a belief and code of existence based on love and concern for one's fellow man, into glorified rituals based on self-aggrandizement, and the robes, costumes and artefacts were, and are, symbols of the different religious standing of members within the hierarchy of the church. Jesus was a humble and self-effacing man, his followers being only interested in what he had to say and not any material attributes they might acquire to portray their allegiance.

The Church of England has become quite a staid and rather dull doctrine by now, and I really do not think the modern generation are drawn to it as in the past. With hindsight, I do not think that I was 'drawn' to it, rather that it was just the way of life - a tradition. Like myself, people are beginning to seek other answers to questions long overdue, and are being drawn towards the 'spiritual', or perhaps losing interest altogether. People now are not sure, particularly the young, what to believe in at all. If there is a God, why does He do nothing in the face of terrible disasters and ghastly wars? However, it is not *God* who creates these events, but man and the nature of our ever-changing planet. Nothing we do will halt climate change – it is a natural phenomenon, and as our surroundings have been constantly changing since the beginning of time as we know it, it would seem we shall all have to adapt accordingly, as previous inhabitants of this planet have done before us.

Our modern-day life has become a rather 'base' existence where no-one is conscious as to who they really are, skimming along the surface, never reaching their souls and a deeper meaning to their lives - living in a world of frenetic obsession with qualifications, rising higher and higher in the world of attainment and competing in a frantic race for the latest technological invention, holiday abroad and villa in the sun, regardless of cost, and bought with the ever-faithful credit card. 'Love Thy Neighbour' does not enter into the lives of most people who, particularly in large towns and cities, live an insular existence where actually to *know* who your neighbour is would be quite unusual! It is sad to think that it would possibly take another war or some cataclysmic event to bring us all together again, and for us all to actually *care* about each other.

What a wonderful accomplishment it would be if we could all come together in the name of 'spirituality' instead of fighting each other in the name of 'religion'. Perhaps some ruthless leader will one day press that fateful button, and it will be too late to learn that we are 'one' – all humans on this planet, equal in merit in our individual groups. I have in mind a scenario where a life form of higher intelligence on another planet is looking down on us and saying "Oh dear, what *do* they think they're doing?"

We need to look inside ourselves for the answer – to raise our game to a higher level, a spiritual level, where each individual takes responsibility for his or her own thoughts and actions; not follow like sheep a doctrine that tells us we are lesser human beings unless we follow its teachings implicitly, or kill in its name.

Finally, to come back to the Bible. A book having been originally written in Aramaic, then Greek, Arabic, translated into Hebrew, and from Hebrew into all our modern languages cannot, in my view, possibly contain an accurate account of events in those early days of Christianity. The populace of that time were also greatly influenced by superstition (one of the greatest forces the world has ever known, and one that several of our popular present day cults and religions are based on!), and the supernatural interpretation of events by soothsayers, being far more ready to believe in this than any logical explanation. Each individual, on recounting an event, would probably have delivered a slightly different rendering of the story from his friend or neighbour, possibly exaggerating and also, quite likely, inventing parts of it to make the listener more enthralled. It might feasibly end up rather like 'Chinese whispers', the original no longer being recognizable. Words and phrases used in ancient times also had an entirely different meaning to the translation of them that we use today. Therefore, if we look at it logically, we have turned possibly inaccurate accounts of events into an exalted and divine 'truth' without question! I also feel that the idea of Heaven being a 'place' where we go when leaving our earthly bodies does not seem plausible, rather that we reach a 'spiritual *haven* of joy and tranquillity', there not being anything remotely physical attached to it. However, as no-one has ever come back we shall never really know. Tunnels of light and immense joy have definitely been experienced though, which gives some indication, and some hope, as to where we might finally come to rest when leaving this world behind. I am sure that it will be a better place than the one in which we now exist.

Continuing with the translation of the Bible and the 'Pesher' (interpretation) technique, I should like to further quote Dr. Thiering:-

"The gospels of the New Testament, and the Book of Revelation, are written in a special language. They make not just an occasional use of symbolism, as most people would concede, but a thoroughgoing, systematic use of sequences of symbols and images, to the extent that a whole new language has been created, and one that needs special information to understand. In that sense, it is a code, although the purpose is not a trivial one.

The purpose was to record a complete and exact history of Jesus and of the events that led to the formation of the Christian Church. But to most of the audience for which it was intended – both then and now – Christianity, with Jesus as a divine human being, was a revelation from heaven, supported by miracles and supernatural events to prove its truth. What they believed they needed was scripture, not a history book.

To those who had lived through the events, however, there was a dilemma. They knew that belief in revelation and miracles was a product of a less mature kind of faith, the faith of a child. It was a necessary step in faith, but it could not be left as the whole content of religion. There was an urgent need to give a means of growing out of fantasy into an adult religion.

The solution came from a definition of scripture that they had developed when they tried to wrestle with the unbelievable parts of the Old Testament. Living at a time of historical crisis for Judaism, they had come to think that their own history was contained within the pages of the Old Testament, but could be seen only because of their special knowledge. When it said, for instance, that 'the righteous will live by faith' and 'the wicked will prosper', it was not simply making general ethical statements, but was giving facts about the leaders. Its 'Pesher' (interpretation) concerns the House of Absalom and the men of its council, who were silent at the chastisement of the Teacher of Righteousness, and they did not help him against the Man of a Lie, who flouted the Law in the midst of their whole congregation.

Scripture, then, in their view, contained hidden historical facts. In the case of the Old Testament, they had read the facts into it; they were not really there. But the definition gave them an ideal way of solving their problems. A new scripture was needed; and, moreover, they needed to record in full detail their history, a history that must, by religious necessity, remain partly secret. This time, the history would be objectively present in their scripture, because they had placed it there.

In the gospels and Acts of the New Testament, they produced a masterpiece. The outline of the real history of Jesus was given on the surface, but dressed in so much apparent miracle that he was presented as the kind of divine human being needed by simple faith. But they set up within it, by symbols, images, double meanings, special meanings, the complete history. It was placed within the stories in a way that was subject to decipherment by those in possession of the special knowledge *required. Everyone who worked on it with the special knowledge would arrive at the same result. It was like a puzzle with a solution, and there could only be one solution.*

One of the methods was to present human beings, religious leaders, in the form of supernatural beings, and real places in the form of heavenly places. Stories such as parables and miracles, apparently dealing with a metaphorical reality or another world, actually record normal human history".

I think it is time to question, not that Jesus lived, but how he lived, what he stood for, how and when he died, and what he would say witnessing our lives today.

The much advanced technology we now have at our fingertips has enabled us to explore, record, decipher, translate and construct the minutiae encapsulated in papyri, tablets, tombs, caves and paintings etc. that have survived to this day, their secrets having lain dormant for thousands of years awaiting the science capable of uncovering them. Coupled with our natural curiosity, and desire to get to the bottom of things, we are now discovering that the 'certainties' we were brought up to believe in are possibly no longer plausible, facts and events having been altered or invented to suit the story-teller and his attentive audience.

It is thought that the seeds of Christianity can be traced back to the Egyptians, the most obvious being the utterance of "Amen" at the end of a prayer. While this is generally thought to come from the Hebrew word meaning 'certainly' or 'so be it', it is equally possible that it refers to the name of the Egyptian Sun God 'Amen-Ra'. Incidentally, Akhenaten was the first person to bring into being the worship of a 'living' entity as opposed to wood and stone idols, this being the worship of the Sun. This happened because Akhenaten realised that a living God would logically have more power than a material man-made object. He had the courage to change the beliefs of his people, albeit that they reverted to the old familiar worship eventually. He nevertheless had the intelligence, foresight and determination, to have attempted this revolutionary turnabout.

The very core beliefs on which both the Roman Catholic Church and the Anglican church exist are based on inaccurate interpretation of the Bible Stories, followers of which have become so accustomed to leading their lives within this framework that to contemplate ever questioning it would seem to be absolute heresy. If this quest for the truth should ever become more forceful, what would be the outcome I wonder? It takes bravery to dare to change peoples' belief and traditional way of life, to question and dissect another's reason for being.

In the 1800's when tombs were being excavated in the Valley of the Kings in Egypt, and when hieroglyphs were first found to mean actual words, the powers that be, the Catholic Church to name but one, were appalled at the thought that these hieroglyphs might reveal that the stories in the Bible had no foundation, that Noah's flood might never have happened, as if it had, the Egyptians would not have survived. This revelation was duly hushed up before it could possibly gather momentum, and so we continue to believe the stories we are told by our revered 'heads' of church.

I consider that we are free to decide who or what guides us through life without mindlessly following another individual's doctrine. The heads of Church, albeit from any religion, automatically seem to command our respect. One has, in my opinion, to *earn* respect by being a sincere and caring person or perhaps someone competent in their field of knowledge or ability. Traditionally we hold our clergy in high regard before we have even met them. We *expect* them to be beyond reproach with an aura of holy righteousness surrounding them. It seems to me to be the ultimate in brainwashing and the biggest con in history! It has, however, managed to control the lives of millions and millions of innocent people who have been coerced into living 'God-fearing' lives without questioning where this doctrine originated or why they should behave in this way. It has, however, swelled the coffers of the Catholic church, and to lesser extent the Anglican, to astronomical proportion.

It would appear that religions have been, and still are, the root of evil. Over the centuries and up to the present time wars are continually being fought in their name, with massive segregation of communities; people ranting at each other and killing each other, in the name of religion. Babies are born to Catholic families unable to sustain them, having been told that it is a 'sin' to practice birth control. In the past this led to unmarried mothers having to give their babies up for adoption through the shame of having allowed themselves to be sullied in this way. This 'law' was passed (for all Catholics to adhere to) by a man of Catholic denomination, unmarried, celibate and not having any first-hand knowledge of sex (supposedly), marriage or birth – not, in actual fact, having much knowledge of life itself; someone who, living in a virtual ivory tower, has done absolutely nothing to gain our respect but nevertheless expects to receive it.

As I write this, the city of London awaits the very controversial visit of Pope Benedict XVI; controversial because, in light of several recent allegations of the sexual abuse of young people by priests, *he has done nothing by way of castigation*, having chosen to ignore any wrongdoing. Those people who suffered abuse under the auspices of the Catholic Church are outraged at his inability to recognize the gravity of these allegations, and are planning a 'protest' against both his visit and the hypocrisy of his professed 'faith'. He will be forced to meet some of them, and presumably to offer some form of 'apology' for the heinous crimes committed by his fellow members.

We basically owe the quality of our lives to our parents, grandparents, and their choice of partners. Clearly parents have a high degree of influence on shaping the character of their children; albeit, our ancestors have just as much direction over the final outcome, the genes being inherited through the generations. Family values are also passed down from generation to generation, the obvious one being the faith of that family. To be seen as a 'churchgoing' family automatically gained respect in the community. We like to *belong*, to be seen to be good, and to feel we are respected for being a sincere participant of an honest and decent society, one of which we are proud to be a member.

THE ONSET OF SLAVERY

Slavery has existed in various forms throughout most of recorded history; from ancient Egypt to the European invasions, Africa in particular has had a long and harrowing history of slavery. In ancient Egypt and Nubia slavery took several forms, from both household and farming to military. Egyptian slaves were also known to be executed to accompany their deceased owner into the afterlife.

Slavery was first introduced in British North America around 1619, when a Dutch ship brought 20 enslaved Africans to the Virginia colony of Jamestown. Nearly 240 years passed before slavery was officially ended in 1865.

In the early days of Christianity black slaves, who had previously been converted to a white 'religion', raised their voices in lyrical supplication to a 'saviour' they had been told would help them. This gave them the reassuring feeling that they were not alone. They needed to believe that their humiliation, degradation and base existence would not last for ever, and that ultimately 'God' would deliver them from a world of brutality and degeneracy into a bright new world where freedom was every person's right, a world where they could hold their heads high, proud in their heritage and the colour of their skins. This faith kept hope in their hearts, which in this particular case, one cannot fault. The only trouble with this is the grossly hypocritical view of most of the slave owners, professing to be devout Christians, living their lives under the auspices of a 'God of Love and Compassion' when inflicting unspeakable atrocities, working and living conditions, on their workforce of black slaves.

With regard to the Southern States of America, the shifting of attitudes towards slavery resulted in profound changes in

Southern society in general, and in religious circles in particular. In the 1780's Methodists had formulated strong rules against slavery, and slaveholders. Slavery was deemed to be *"contrary to the laws of God, man and nature, and hurtful to society, contrary to the dictates of conscience and pure religion"*. By 1784 Methodists were so bold as to say that they *"promised to excommunicate all Methodists not freeing their slaves within two years"*. By 1820 however, the Methodist church in the South was increasingly at one with its culture on the issue of race, and was advocating a 'Mission to the Slaves'.

As the conflict over slavery heated up, a great fear enveloped whites. Afraid for their lives, their investments, the civil peace, and the preservation of the South's way of life, whites demanded laws curtailing the rights of African-Americans to assemble, to worship, to become literate, and to do much more, except under strictly controlled circumstances. At the same time this fear and anxiety was producing an outpouring of concern to make Christians of the slaves in the hope that they might learn to turn the other cheek, and to accept their lot in life.

In the early decades of the nineteenth century, Christianity had made little or no impression among the black population for fear that they might take literally such narratives as the Exodus. But as this 'crisis of fear' spread across the South, suddenly rather impressive efforts were made to address the 'needs' of the souls of black folk. These were well organized evangelistic endeavours, particularly in those areas with large plantations. Congregations stepped up their appeals, and refined their approaches to African-Americans. Preachers and planters alike urged them to fill the galleries, and special seating was set aside for these honoured guests. Some owners were even motivated to build 'praise houses' on their land, and recruited black preachers to proclaim the Lord's name (as long as a white foreman was present to monitor things so that they did not get out of hand). Large slaveholders worked to comprise a Christian primer for slaves to instil teachings that were designed as a response to the portents of revolution, and to serve as preventive measures to any insurrection.

This is not to say that the whole effort to evangelize the slaves was motivated by a concern for safety. There were certainly a number of whites who cared about blacks, both as persons possessing immortal souls, and as friends with names. Many others saw the mission to the slaves as an unfolding of God's divine plan and these early evangelistic efforts as the first step in a long process that would eventually lead to the converting of the 'heathen of the dark continent'. But there were many others who sought to pacify and comfort the slaves, to make them more dutiful and servile, and to defer any gratification they might have longed for in this life to the next.

The motives of White Southerners appeared decidedly mixed.

Often there was a genuine recognition of the human needs of African Americans, but rarely would the members of the 'Ruling Race' overlook the unique caste and economic status of black people. Very little of what the white church attempted and accomplished from 1830 to the Civil War remained free of racial and interracial considerations.

THE RELIGIOUS LIFE OF THE SLAVES

Various plantation owners expressed concern that 'African superstitions' had not been wholly discarded. Witchcraft, alleged superstitions, and fetishist practices were often cited as evidence that the plantation slave refused to acknowledge Christianity.

Although the African's world was populated by a legion of magical spirits, most tribes believed in a Supreme Being who was viewed as a creator, giver of rain, sunshine and nature in general – one who existed by himself. All of life was sacred, nor was there any sense of distinction between this life and the life to come. Long before their contact with whites, Africans were a strongly religious, and deeply spiritual people. These long held beliefs were not too dissimilar to the Christian teaching, therefore African's took to conversion without much resistence.

However, Africans also bequeathed something back to the evangelical tradition, there being some evidence that suggests some whites copied certain practices of black worshippers. Shouting in worship, for example, was one such borrowing. Many blacks looked down on whites who shouted in worship, being poor copies of themselves.

When African-Americans held their own services, they added their own unique styles to the white religious legacy. In doing so, they created an 'invisible institution', a church that was their own. The rituals and dogmas performed during the early history of slavery were often described as Voodoo, Witchcraft and superstitions. Whites often feared these 'pagan practices' and were threatened by them. As a result, the whites vociferously encouraged the eradication of such practices, and many were lost within a generation.

One of the profound differences between worship by the blacks and worship by the whites was the expressiveness of spirit that came to characterize black religion. While the White Methodists and Baptists were also expressive, their outpourings did nothing to match the black wailings of despair or shouts of pure joy! Bad news of one's eternal damnation called for a groaning and wailing befitting one's anguish and sorrow. Good news however, of God's gracious offer of forgiveness through the love of Christ's sacrificial death, was received with shouts of joy and praise for blessed release. This expression of feeling meant that most blacks felt inhibited in white churches, even though many accompanied the whites at the alter. Most African-Americans found that their spiritual needs would be met by meeting in secret. The conditions in which they lived were evil, but they did not see themselves as being evil. The spiritual music composed and sung by them was every bit as direct, heartfelt and meaningful as Black Preaching. Such hymns as 'Swing low, Sweet Chariot' conveys a message that few whites heard; a fundamental equality of persons - God welcomes both whites and blacks into 'heaven'. Their religion dealt with life as they lived it, being about pain, sorrow, sin and shortcoming, forgiveness and joy, praise and thanksgiving, grace and hope. In some ways, church life proved to be more important than family life in the African-American household.

RELIGION IN THE '60's

Throughout the 1950's religion in families was taken for granted (those who believed the Christian teachings), and children followed their parents' example. Religion was a steadfast, safe and grounding experience for all. However, as this generation of children reached their 'teens they began to feel stifled and oppressed and found themselves looking for something they could call their own, something entirely different, and the 'Hippie' era was born. The word 'hippie' comes from the word 'hip', meaning 'aware of' or 'knowing'. The nickname 'hippie' was coined from the beatniks in San Francisco. They gave the name 'hippies' to the younger generation of college students who looked up to and followed the older 'beatniks'. Beatniks were young people who rejected traditional ways of living, dressing and behaving. They read poetry to each other in groups, the majority smoking a large amount of marijuana - the forerunners of the 'hippies'.

Many hippies experimented with drugs, particularly marijuana and L.S.D., to expand their consciousness. This movement was led by an American, Timothy Leary, who encouraged young people to "turn on, tune in, and drop out". Hippies often lived in communes and had open sexual relationships, or 'free love'. Vegetarianism and environmentalism were introduced to mainstream America by the hippies. They practiced spiritualism, Eastern religion, alternative medicine, transcendental meditation and astrology, which led to the decade's nickname 'the age of Aquarius'.

The hippie movement was partially a reaction to the Vietnam War and the draft. Young men burnt their draft cards or fled to Canada. The anti-war, pacifist motto of the hippies was "make love, not war". Protests of the war were common, especially on college campuses. Women's rights and racial equality were also very important issues that the hippies supported. However, many hippies, while politically aware, chose to 'drop out' of society instead of engaging actively in protests and political struggles.

They developed a distinct way of dressing. Many men grew their hair long (an attempt to follow the style of the original advocate of peace, Jesus), challenging traditional conventions. Unisex style clothing was also popular. Popular trends were ethnic clothing, love beads, bell bottoms, granny glasses, 'Jesus' sandals, and flowing silhouettes. As a rejection of conventionalism hippies often wore second hand clothes or made their own. Their music reflected their beliefs, that of non-violence, peace and spirituality, and this message spread rapidly throughout the Western world, young people in Britain becoming fascinated with this unconventional and tranquil way of life. Eastern religions became popular, and Indian gurus, Tibetan lamas, Japanese Zen masters, and other Eastern 'sages' came to the West and found a host of ready disciples who made them successful beyond their dreams. Young people travelled all over the world, even to the heights of the Himalayas, to find the wisdom, the teacher, or the drug that would bring them the 'peace' and 'freedom' they sought.

The 1970's produced a third generation, succeeding the hippies, who were outwardly quieter, with less flamboyant behaviour and fewer demonstrations. For many of this newer generation the religious 'search' had ended; they had found an Eastern religion to their liking and were now seriously occupied in practicing it. A number of Eastern religious movements have already become 'native' to the West, especially in America. There are now Buddhist monasteries composed entirely of Western converts, and for the first time there have appeared American, British and other practicing Western gurus and Zen masters.

JOHN LENNON and 'The Beatles'

One of the most iconic figures from the '60's to have retained recognition is John Lennon. His very controversial views regarding Christianity shook the Western world, and particularly America. In the newspaper, the London Evening Standard, he is quoted as saying :- *"Christianity will go. It will vanish and shrink. I'm right, and I will be proved right. We're more popular than Jesus now. I don't know which will go first, rock'n'roll or Christianity. Jesus was all right, but his disciples were thick and ordinary"*.

John would be asked many times during The Beatles' 1966 tour of North America, to explain and clarify what he had intended to say. The outrage that Americans showed came mainly from the 'bible belt'. A minority of Americans resorted to action, burning records of the Beatles around radio stations, and there were even protests from the Ku Klux Klan, involving anonymous death threats.

John is again quoted as saying:- *"My views are only from what I've read or observed of Christianity and what it was, and what it has been, or what it could be. It just seems to me to be shrinking. I'm not knocking it or saying it's bad. I'm just saying it seems to be shrinking and losing contact"*.

During an interview with 'Look' magazine in 1966:- *"I said we were more popular than Jesus, which is a fact. I believe Jesus was right. They're all saying the same thing, and I believe it. I believe what Jesus actually said – the basic things he laid down about love and goodness – and not what people say he said"*.

In 1968 The Beatles went to India to study Transcendental Meditation with the Maharishi Mahesh Yogi, whom they had previously met in London. By this time they had achieved worldwide fame and wealth, and now wished to explore their 'inner selves', and their place in the universe. John Lennon, in particular, found real peace of mind from the techniques he learned from the Maharishi. However, he is said to have questioned the Maharishi's intentions where the women of the party were involved, as it seemed apparent that he seemed more than a little interested in them!

They spent several weeks at the Maharishi's ashram with other superstars such as Donovan, Mia Farrow and others. However, they began to feel that they were being taken advantage of, with regard to their popularity and wealth. They left and returned to England. George Harrison continued his studies and embraced the Hindu philosophy completely.

A quote from John Lennon's personal tarot card reader, John Green, says:- *"He was not of vague appearance. He was quite startlingly 'there'. To say that it was an 'aura', not so much that, as just the energy field around him"*.

On the evening of December 8ᵗʰ 1980, John Lennon was tragically murdered in front of his apartment building in New York. His assassin was Mark David Chapman. Chapman showed absolutely no emotion as he calmly sat down and waited for police to arrest him. He pleaded guilty and was sentenced to 20 years to life in Attica State Prison.

John Lennon's death remains a total mystery to this day, although some say that it could have been a conspiracy, and that his death was orchestrated by the CIA. His private life was intensely investigated by the New York Police Dept., his 'phone records, particularly long distance, being minutely examined. The Police Department sent detectives to Atlanta and Honolulu to investigate Chapman for any sign as to his part in a conspiracy, to no avail, as this was denied. Chapman is now viewed as being mentally unstable. The file of one of the most notorious murder cases in New York's history remains to this day inaccessible to Freedom of Information Act inquiries.

THE PRACTICE OF WITCHCRAFT

Ancient tribal witches within most cultures across the world, from the Celtic druids to the Native American shaman, consisted of spirituality and 'magic' centred around the use of herbs, bestowing curses or blessings and affecting weather patterns. Until the Christian Church gained enormous control throughout the world, these practices remained. The Inquisition and the Crusades transformed all non-Christian practices into one category, which later became known as 'witchcraft'.

Witchcraft is very poorly understood. Although witches today believe that witchcraft history pre-dates Christianity, most historians and theologians disagree. Pagans connect modern witchcraft with ancient pre-Christian beliefs. However, historians define modern witchcraft as an invention of the Christian Inquisition, in which the Church redefined all pre-Christian faiths throughout Europe. Historians recognize that before the Christian Church grouped all non-Christian faiths into one category, all of these religious practices were very different from one another.

These traditions, herbalism, divination and magic, existed well into the Middle Ages. Pagan cults included their own priests and priestesses, such as the Celtic priests who were called 'Druids'. This Celtic cult was a very common European paganism centred around the worship of trees. The term 'wizard' has its roots in the Pagan priests who had gone into hiding, yet travelled the countryside to perform services for practitioners scattered throughout the land.

The image of the 'witch' being an old hag originated from the old female peasants who used pagan ceremonies and spells into the first few centuries of Christianity when pagan practice was not yet a crime. These practices were usually rooted in old tribal beliefs centred around nature, weather and primitive spiritual practices.

The Celts were a deeply spiritual people, who worshipped both a god and a goddess. They worshipped many aspects of the 'One Creative Life Source' and honoured the presence of the 'Divine Creator' in all of nature. Like many tribes the world over, they believed in reincarnation. After death, they went to the Summerland for rest and renewal while awaiting rebirth.

They were a people living between 700 BC and 100 AD. Believed to be descendants of Indo-Europeans, the Celts were a dynamic and intelligent people – gifted artists, musicians, storytellers, expert farmers and fierce warriors. They were much feared by their adversaries, the Romans, who eventually adopted a number of their customs and traditions.

The months of the Celtic year were named after trees. The Celtic new year began at Samhain, which means 'summers end', and was the final harvest of the year. This was also their 'Festival of the Dead', where they honoured their ancestors and deceased loved ones. Many contemporary Halloween customs originate from Samhain. The Winter Solstice celebrated the annual rebirth of the Sun. Our Christmas customs today are similar to this ancient celebration. Around the beginning of February came Imbolg, a time when domesticated animals began to give birth. The Spring Equinox and Beltaine, sometimes called 'May Day', were fertility festivals. The Summer Solstice, known as Lughnassa, celebrated the glory of the Sun and the powers of nature. Lughnassa, the Fall Equinox, and Samhain, were considered as Celtic harvest festivals.

THE DRUIDS

The Druids were the priests of the Celtic religion. They remained in power through the fourth century AD, three centuries after the Celts' defeat at the hand of the Romans. The Druids were priests, teachers, judges, astrologers, healers and bards. They became indispensable to the political leaders, giving them considerable power and influence. They were peacemakers, and were able to pass from one warring tribe to another unharmed. It took twenty years of intense study to become a Druid.

The religious beliefs and practices of the Celts grew into what later became known as Paganism. The word Pagan is derived from the Latin word Paganus, meaning 'country dweller', emulating their love for the land and their holding such things as the oak tree and mistletoe sacred.

The term 'witch', which means to twist or bend, originates from the Anglo-Saxon word 'wicca', which is derived from the word 'wicce', which means wise. It is said that the origins of the witch date back thousands of years, to the days when the goddess was worshipped and humanity had great reverence for the powers of nature and for women as creators of new life. In the 'New Age' philosophy, this relates to the concept of 'Gaia', or 'Mother Earth', which views planet earth as essentially a living being.

The founding of the Inquisition and the Crusades was initially directed against Muslims, but then became focused on 'heretics' within the Church's own ranks. As heretics became more difficult to locate, Pope Innocent VIII eventually added those who practiced 'witchcraft' into the same category as heretics, and made them subject to arrest and trial. The Church taught that witches worshipped a false deity of witchcraft that never existed before, known today as Satanism or 'devil worship'. During this time the Church grouped all religions, including Pagans, Jews, Gypsies and others, under the category of 'witchcraft'.

The Inquisition subjected those accused of 'witchcraft' to horrific punishment. Men, women and children were tortured and killed in unmentionable ways. At the end of this dark period of witchcraft, over 50,000 people had been murdered for being labelled a 'heretic' or 'witch'.

In recent history, from the 1920's through to the 1950's, a new form of witchcraft has emerged, created from remnants of those earlier primitive pagan beliefs and practices. Intellectuals throughout Europe began attempting to explain these phenomena, and eventually created our present religion of 'witchcraft'.

Today, throughout the world, witchcraft remains a practice that is growing in popularity, but also greatly misunderstood. Practices that include divination, clairvoyance, herbalism and other activities, now termed 'new age', have a witchcraft history that originates from the new witchcraft that was reborn throughout the early 1900's.

THE PRACTICE OF VOODOO

The practice of 'voodoo' presents us with the outcome of life events through the connection with nature, spirits, and ancestors. True rituals are held behind closed doors, as to execute these in showy fashion would be considered disrespectful to the spirits. Voodoo rituals include readings, spiritual baths, specially devised diets and prayers. They are frequently used to cure anxiety, addictions, depression, loneliness and other ailments, The practice of Voodoo is probably as old as the African continent itself. The word Voodoo means 'God Creator' or 'Great Spirit'. Human sacrifices, dripping blood, vampires and devil worship have all contributed to our fascination of Hollywood movies and horror stories. It is practiced by millions throughout the world, in Africa, the Caribbean, Central, North and South America, in various forms, and often with elements of Catholicism mixed in. However, its main purpose is to heal.

When the slave trade first began, slaves were taken from the West Coast of Africa and the Congo region. They brought with them their beliefs and regional practices. Many were first brought to the Caribbean islands to work the plantations and be forcibly Christianized, their owners not recognizing the mystical qualities of their native ceremonies, considering them to be nothing more than savages. Amidst broken tribes and families they found unity and solace in God and ancient rituals.

The Voodoos believe in the existence of one supreme God, omnipotent yet untouchable force. Below this almighty God, Spirits or Loa rule over the family in matters of world affairs, of family, love, happiness, health, wealth, work, fairness and the harvest or hunt, and offerings are made to the appropriate Loa to ensure success in those areas. The Loa also manifest through elements of nature such as the wind and rain, lightning and thunder, the river, the ocean, springs and lakes, the sky, the sun, certain animals, trees and stones. Every element of nature, animal, tree, plant, fruit or vegetable is sacred to a certain Loa or Orisha.

They understood the similarities between their beliefs and those of the Catholics; the Catholics praying to their Saints to intercede to a higher God in their favour. Elaborate ceremonies and costumes of the church also had great appeal for the Africans.

Voodoo was brought to the French colony Louisiana through the slave trade, the majority of African slaves coming from Benin, West Africa, bringing with them their cultural practices, language, and religious beliefs, rooted in spirit and ancestor worship. Their knowledge of herbs, poisons, and the ritual use of charms and amulets, intended to protect oneself or possibly to harm others, became key elements of Louisiana Voodoo.

The practice of making and wearing charms and amulets for protection, healing, or the harm of others was a key aspect to early Louisiana Voodoo. The *ouanga*, a charm used to poison an enemy, contained the poisonous roots of the figure maudit tree, brought from Africa and preserved in the West Indies. The ground up root was combined with other elements such as bones, nails, roots, holy water, holy candles, holy incense, holy bread, or crucifixes. The administrator of the ritual frequently evoked protection from Allah, the Christian God, and Jesus Christ. This openness of African belief allowed for the adoption of Catholic practices into Louisiana Voodoo.

Originally, the spirits that presided over every day matters of life, such as family, love, and justice, were called by their African names, but once French Creole replaced native African languages, their original names were no longer used. The spirits then adopted the names of Catholic Saints, each spirit being paired with a Saint in charge of similar spheres of life.

Catholic traditions, such as prayers including the Hail Mary and the Lord's Prayer, baptism, and the sign of the cross, were incorporated into Voodoo practices.

During the nineteenth century, Voodoo queens became central figures to Voodoo in the United States. These queens presided over ceremonial meetings and ritual dances, also receiving payment for administering charms, amulets, and magical powders guaranteed to cure ailments, grant desires, and to harm or destroy one's enemies.

The Voodoo Queen of New Orleans in the 1830's was Marie Laveau. The news of her powers spread, and she was able to overthrow the other Queens of New Orleans. Acting as an oracle, she conducted private rituals behind her cottage on St. Ann Street of the New Orleans French Quarter, performing exorcisms and offering sacrifices to the spirits. Marie, being a devout Catholic, encouraged her followers to attend Catholic Mass, the influence of her Catholic beliefs further facilitating the adoption of Catholic practices into the Voodoo belief system. Marie Laveau continues to be a central figure of Louisiana Voodoo and of New Orleans culture, gamblers shouting her name for luck when throwing their dice, and multiple tales of sightings of the Voodoo queen have been told.

The slave community quickly acquired a strong presence in Louisiana. As the colony was not a stable society when slaves arrived, it allowed African culture to maintain a prominent position in the community. Slaves were owned by only a few white settlers, facilitating the preservation of African culture.

During the 1930's original Voodoo went underground when New Orleans became a thriving tourist attraction. The misconception developed that the principal elements of Voodoo were hexing and sticking pins into dolls. This came about from the viewing of the 1932 Hollywood film 'White Zombie'. Voodoo practitioners were inundated with requests for various charms, 'Gris-gris', and powders etc. Those in search of a fortune began charging for such favours, as true followers never did.

The Voodoo spell known as the 'cure-all' was very popular among followers. This was a spell that could solve all problems. There were different recipes for cure-all; one recipe was to mix jimson weed with sulphur and honey. The mixture was then placed in a glass which was rubbed against a black cat, and then the mixture was slowly sipped.

The Voodoo doll is a form of 'Gris-gris', an example of sympathetic magic. Contrary to popular belief, Voodoo dolls are usually used to 'bless' instead of 'curse'. The purpose of sticking pins in the doll is not to cause pain in the person the doll is associated with, but rather to pin a picture of a person or a name to the doll, which traditionally represents a spirit. The 'Gris-gris' is then performed from one of four categories, love, power and domination, luck and finance, and uncrossing.

The main aim of Louisiana Voodoo today is to serve others and influence seeking to help the poor, the hungry, and the sick as Marie Laveau once did.

The similarities between Voodoo and Catholicism are what kept African beliefs from dying out, and historically, there has been little hostility between followers of Catholicism and Voodoo in New Orleans. Although Voodoo later experienced opposition from Protestant churches, its relationship to the Catholic Church has always been amicable.

GARGOYLES

The earliest known existence of these grotesquely carved human/animal figures is in 13th century France. The word gargoyle comes from the old French word 'gargouille' meaning throat or gullet, hence the origin of the word 'gargle'. This word was originally used with reference to the drains on the rooftops of medieval cathedrals, which were later carved to form animals and grotesque human/mythical forms etc.. They were designed to act as a spout to throw rainwater clear of a building, and it is said that no two gargoyles are alike, stonemasons etc. having free choice over their design. All, however, possessing hideous, gaping mouths to enable the water to freely flow. Some say they were meant to ward off the devil, whilst others believe that they were meant to warn parishioners of the perils of evil. Perhaps the church wanted to convey a terrifying impression of Hell, and so to enforce the impression that there was safety and sanctuary inside the church. Gargoyles which combine several different animals are known as chimeras. Ancient myths often tell of beings with human heads and animal or bird bodies, such as the 'sphinx' or 'mermaid'. Originally made of wood or terracotta, they were painted and sometimes even gilded, and then in the Medieval Gothic period they were made of stone. The gargoyles which appeared inside churches were predominantly limestone and marble, although metals such as lead were also used.

These frightening and grotesque sculptures are a fascinating element of Medieval Architecture, and although mostly associated with churches, are also to be seen in English Gothic castles to frighten off their enemies!

Although their origin is associated with France, in actual fact gargoyles can be traced back to ancient Egyptian, Roman and Greek architecture.

GALILEO

Over hundreds of years both Christians and atheists have clashed over trying to prove either that God miraculously created man and the universe, or that their origins are the result of science. It is said that Galileo was tortured and imprisoned by the Catholic church, condemned for heresy, and forced to denounce his scientific work.

Galileo Galilei is generally credited as being the first person to use the telescope for astronomical purposes, and was one of the great instigators of the 17th century science revolution. Although being a believer of the Catholic faith and a member of its church, he did his best not to mention religion wherever possible in his scientific writings. He did recognize, however, that religion was one of the dominant powers of the era, and he sometimes tried to use this fact to his advantage, particularly taking relish in using religion to contradict itself!

Galileo used his intellectual works as a safe haven from the pressures of the outside world. In this way he was assured that scientists were his only real audience, and that there was no need to include religion into his writing to appease anyone. He saw no reason to compare his work to anything that might be written in the Bible. There has been no proof given as to how Galileo really felt about the relationship between science and religion. He knew that religion was an integral part of nearly every single person's life in that era, and so he reasoned that religious arguments held more weight than scientific proofs among the 'common man'. He also acknowledged that certain passages within the Bible may have been simplified for the benefit of easy understanding. It also seems apparent that he believed religion had no place in the scientific world.

Galileo was an Illuminatus, a member of the Order of the Illuminati (the "enlightened"). This was an Order formed to oppose the dictatorship of the Catholic church over the people of Rome. He believed that science did not undermine the existence of God, but rather reinforced it. He held that rather than being enemies both science and religion should be allies, the same story being told in two different languages, and tried to soften the antagonistic approach that the church held with regard to science.

The conflict between Galileo and the Catholic Church surfaced in 1633 when formal inquisition proceedings were set in motion against him. He could either revoke his support of his scientific findings or be tortured and presumably killed. He chose the former, under sufferance. He was instructed not to teach, in any way whatsoever, his beliefs in science.

Galileo's arrest considerably affected the Illuminati, the majority of their members going underground to form a different sect. The Catholic church captured and tortured several members, branding them with the sign of the cross. Scientists were also murdered and deposited in the streets of Rome as a warning to those who might contemplate joining the Order.

From the evidence he has left behind, it would seem that Galileo wished that religion had never come about. As religion *does* exist, he wanted to have as little to do with it as possible.

Order of the "ILLUMINATI"

The Order of the Illuminati was formed in the 1500's when a group of enlightened men in Rome decided to fight back against the Catholic Church. Physicists, astronomers and mathematicians came together, meeting in secret to share their concerns with regard to the power the church held, and its inaccurate teachings. Calling themselves "the enlightened ones" they were the first group to challenge the so-called "truth" that the Catholic Church laid down, and instructed that people should unquestioningly believe.

The Illuminati virtually rebuilt London after the Great Fire in 1666. Nicholas Hawksmoor was an English architect of the time, and was instrumental in the design of some of the new buildings including six churches, St. Alfege's Church, Greenwich, St. George's Church, Bloomsbury, Christ Church, Spitalfields, St. George's in the East, Wapping, St. Mary Woolnoth and St. Anne's, Limehouse, with St. Paul's Cathedral at the very centre, designed by Christopher Wren, Nicholas Hawksmoor also having contributed to the design. Other buildings of note that he was instrumental in establishing were Blenheim Palace and Castle Howard. The churches are so placed that when linked by triangles form a pentagram, St. Paul's in the centre, being the very heart of London. The Illuminati also hid their symbols in plain sight, such as the obelisks in both London and New York, the pyramid in Paris, and many other evocative symbols in the two cities. Paris was considered the epi-centre for both the Freemasons and the Illuminati, also many secret societies had 'lodges' in the city; many top-ranking Freemasons being members of the Illuminati.

Within the academic world word spread and the brotherhood grew to include academics all over Europe. Many of its members were inclined to combat the church's hold with violence, but their most senior member, Galileo, was against it, being a pacifist. The church retaliated against this now powerful Order with the violence that Galilieo had wished to avoid. Scientists were tortured and murdered, their chests being branded with the sign of the cross. As a result of this, members went underground, connecting with occultists, alchemists, mystics and the darker elements of humanity, vowing to re-group in a more powerful and determined force, to take revenge on the Catholic Church. They were considered by the Vatican to be the most dangerous anti-Christian force in the world.

This new Order was founded by five men in Bavaria on May 1, 1776. The goals of the organisation were to eliminate superstition, prejudice, to support women's education and equality, and to counteract the Roman Catholic Church's dominance over government, philosophy and science, being modelled largely on the Freemasons. In 1777 Duke Karl Theodor became ruler of Bavaria, and by 1784 his government had banned all secret societies, including the Illuminati. By 1785 it was no longer safe to be associated with the Illuminati, at least in Bavaria.

There is no evidence that the original Illuminati survived its suppression in 1785, or have amassed any significant political power, though several present-day groups claim to descend from the original Order. However, some theorists contend that historical events such as the battle of Waterloo, the French Revolution and also the assassination of President John F. Kennedy were orchestrated by the Illuminati.

CHARLES DARWIN

Charles Robert Darwin was the first of the evolutionary biologists, originating the concept of natural selection. He was born in Shrewsbury, the son of a doctor and the daughter of Josiah Wedgwood. He first studied medicine at Edinburgh but decided he was not cut out for a medical career. Instead he was transferred to Cambridge where he studied biology under Prof. John Henslow. Through the efforts of Prof. Henslow, he was able to obtain an invitation to board the *Beagle*, which was being outfitted by the Admiralty for a voyage to the South Seas. The plans for the voyage of the *Beagle* were to take place over the best part of five years (1831-36) and was to visit the southern islands, the South American coast and Australia. Darwin's purpose on board was to serve as geologist, botanist, zoologist, and general man of science. It was quite rare, in those days, to accept anyone on board who could read and write, let alone such educated person as Darwin clearly was.

On his return in 1840, he published his research under the heading *'Zoology of the Beagle'* :-

"When on board H.M.S. Beagle as naturalist, I was much struck with certain facts in the distribution of the organic beings inhabiting South America, and in the geological relations of the present to the past inhabitants of that continent. These facts, as will be seen in the latter chapters of this volume, seemed to throw some light on the origin of species – that mystery of mysteries, as it has been called by one of our greatest philosophers. On my return home, it occurred to me, in 1837, that something might perhaps be made out on this question by patiently accumulating and reflecting on all sorts of facts which could possibly have any bearing on it. After five years' work I allowed myself to speculate on the subject, and drew up some short notes; these I enlarged in 1844 into a sketch of the

conclusions, which then seemed to me probable; from that period to the present day I have steadily pursued the same object. I hope that I may be excused for entering on these personal details, as I give them to show that I have not been hasty in coming to a decision".

On taking the podium to deliver his speech he said:-

"A man has no reason to be ashamed of having an ape for his grandfather. If there were an ancestor whom I should feel shame in recalling, it would be a man of restless and versatile intellect, who, not content with success in his own sphere of activity, plunges into scientific questions with which point at issue he has no real acquaintance, only to obscure them by an aimless rhetoric, and distract the attention of his hearers from them by eloquent digressions and skilled appeals to religious prejudice".

The theory of evolution is no longer just a theory. There is an overwhelming amount of evidence to substantiate Darwin's theory. He discovered *natural laws*. The theory though, contrary to popular belief, has been around since Aristotle and Lucretius; Darwin's contribution is that he gathered indisputable evidence. He set forth a theory on how evolution works, the theory of natural selection. Life has come into being existing and depending on the force of natural selection, in the same way that the earth is in orbit and depends on the force of gravity. If this idea of natural selection holds good, then animals, plants and man himself have become what they are by natural causes, and by all accounts, man is not finished in his progression. *He has the possibility of further progressive evolution in front of him.*

Through our understanding of DNA we now have a much more sophisticated view of genetically inherited traits, which provides a much stronger scientific basis for Darwin's 150 year old theory.

NATIVE AMERICAN BELIEFS

Native American Indians believed in spirits which could bring good or evil to their tribe, in close connection with nature. They feared the swirling depths of water during a flood, believing that the waves and currents were evil spirits, and they relied on nature's resources to keep them alive. The plains men, women and children lived in harmony with nature, believing that killing for sport or pleasure was wasteful and an insult to the Great Spirit.

The Great Spirit was called 'Wakan Tanka' by the Sioux who believed that success and failure in hunting or farming were dictated by him. Changes of season or the weather were dictated by this mysterious Great Spirit and that if people trod carefully on earth they could expect a generous reward in the afterlife. They also believed that the sun, the earth, the sky, the mountains, the animals and all things around them possessed a spirit which they should worship. All of these spirits were controlled by 'Wakan Tanka', which means 'great mystery'. Prayers, offerings and religious ceremonies were extremely important, and the Sioux spent much of their lives trying to please the spirits and enlist their help. Their days began with prayers and by giving thanks, this sometimes included making offerings of their best dogs and horses, or their most beautiful possessions, to show their humble appreciation and to keep the spirits happy.

Of course the Sioux, and all other tribes, are renowned for their spiritual dances, one of the most popular being the 'Sun Dance'. This was the most sacred of their dances and was known to them as 'Looking at the Sun'. This dance was performed to make sure that the power of the sun would come back each day. This was the highest form of worship for the

Sioux and involved a considerable amount of pain for those taking part.

The 'Sun Dance' was performed by men continually dancing round a central pole for up to four days and nights. The torture involved was suffered individually – men having wooden skewers driven through the skin on their chests. These skewers were then tied with rope to the central pole. The men had to dance until the skin had been ripped free. Some men actually had skewers placed on their faces for the same purpose.

The Sioux and other tribes believed that some people in the tribe were especially gifted at contacting the spirits, and each tribe had a medicine man, second only to the chief. This man was in charge of all the ceremonies and was believed to have very strong magical powers. He was expected to predict the future, cast love spells, heal the sick, advise the tribe and protect them from evil spirits.

To contact these spirits the Medicine Men would use music, fasting and herbs to fall into a trance. As they moved into the dark and obscure world of the spirits they left their bodies behind and began to utter strange words, which were eagerly listened to by the rest of the tribe who waited for guidance. Most Medicine Men had good knowledge of herbs and plants which were used to cure sickness, not all help coming through spirits.

Because they lived so close to nature, all Native American people knew that death was never far away from either hunger, disease, or their enemies. Individual tribes adapted their burial customs to the regional environments into which they migrated. They believed that the souls of the dead passed into a spirit world and became part of the spiritual forces that influenced every aspect of their lives. A number of tribes believed in two souls, one that died when the body died and one that wandered on to eventually die later.

Burial customs varied from tribe to tribe, disposing their dead in a variety of different ways. Some placed their dead in lavishly furnished tombs; others simply left their dead in the open frozen waste in which they lived, for wild animals to demolish. The North Eastern Iroquois saved skeletons of the deceased for a final mass burial that included burying with them furs and ornaments for the dead spirits' use in the afterlife; coastal tribes put their dead in canoes fastened to poles; during outbreaks of diseases such as smallpox leading to the sudden death of many tribe members, the survivors would bury the corpses in mass graves or throw them into the river.

Among many tribes mourners would cut their hair, discard personal ornaments or black their faces to honour the dead, engaging in long wailing ceremonies. The nomadic tribes in the Great Plains region buried their dead, if the ground proved to be soft, or left them on high tree platforms or scaffolds, if the ground were too hard to penetrate. Central and South Atlantic tribes embalmed and mummified the bodies.

The Apache and Navajo feared the ghosts of the dead, believing them to resent the living. The Apache buried their corpses quickly, and burned the dead person's house and belongings, leaving the mourning family to purify itself ritually and move to a new site to escape the ghost of the dead family member. Navajos who were exposed to a corpse had to undergo a long ritual purification.

When English and European immigrants arrived on the North American continent they encountered tribes of Native American Indians whose appearance, lifestyle and spiritual beliefs vastly differed from their own. These settlers needed land for their farms, and they sought it by sale, treaty or by using force. Between the 1830 Indian Removal Act and 1850, the United States government used forced treaties or physical force to move approximately 100,000 Native American Indians living east of the Mississippi River, west to Indian Territory in what is now Oklahoma. This triggered a seven-year war that ended in 1843. The trails the Indians followed became known as the 'Trail of Tears'.

Many Cherokees began adopting some of the cultural patterns of the white settlers by the 1820's. They copied the new crop and farming techniques, and some Cherokee farms grew into small plantations, worked by African slaves. They encouraged missionaries to build schools to educate their children in the English language, and to promote literacy. Not all of the tribal elders approved of the ways in which many in the tribe adopted white cultural practices, and removed themselves from its influence, to retreat into what is now north western Arkansas. Others spoke out against this interference of their culture and of the participation of the Cherokee in Christian churches and schools, predicting an end to their own traditional practices. They believed that these adherences to white culture would destroy the tribe's hold on the land.

Most Cherokees wanted to stay on their land, and an old Cherokee Chief summed up their view:-

"My sun of existence is now fast approaching to its setting, and my aged bones will soon be laid underground, and I wish them laid in the bosom of this earth we have received from our fathers, who had it from the Great Being above".

Federal troops began to move the Cherokees into stockades, and in spite of a warning to troops to treat them kindly, the roundup proved to be extremely harrowing. They were dragged from their houses, unable to take anything with them, leaving in the clothes they stood up in, and encamped at the forts and military posts all over the nation. Their houses were left for others to plunder. Three groups left one summer, travelling by boat, train and wagon. Sanitation was deplorable, and food, medicine, clothing and coffins for the dead were in short supply. Many died as disease swept through the camps, often as a result of drinking contaminated water. Most Native American Indians were moved and relocated in this way.

One Cherokee survivor later recalled:-

"Long time we travel on way to new land. People feel bad when they leave Old Nation. Women cry and made sad wails. Children cry and many men cry, and all look sad like when friends die, but they say nothing and just put heads down and keep on go towards West. Many days pass and people die very much".

THE AMISH

The Amish are one of several denominations that developed out of the Radical Reformation in 16th century Europe. The Anabaptists, as the radical reformers came to be called, differed from mainstream Protestants in their rejection of all church authority, belief that a church consists only of baptized believers and rejection of infant baptism. Anabaptist denominations include the Mennonites, Hutterites and the Amish. They originated in Switzerland, with the strict teachings of Jacob Amman that led to a split from other Mennonites in 1693. They are especially known for their separation from society and their rejection of most modern technology.

Amish communities spread to Alsace, Germany, Russia and Holland, but there are none remaining in Europe today. Most emigrated to North America in the 19th and 20th centuries, in large part to avoid religious persecution and compulsory military service, first settling in Pennsylvania, where a large settlement exists today. In 1850 a schism arose between the Old Order Amish and the 'New Order' Amish, the new order accepting social change and technological innovation, but retaining most of the old Amish practices. There are now approximately 200,000 Old Order Amish living in more than 200 settlements in the United States and Canada, the largest communities being in Ohio, Indiana, Iowa, Illinois, Kansas, Wisconsin, Missouri and Minnesota.

As conservative Protestants, the Amish value the Bible alone as their source of religious authority, though in most Amish homes a special place is reserved for the 'Martyr's Mirror', a book chronicling Amish history and honouring the many Amish, Mennonites, and Anabaptists who died for their faith.

The Amish have a revulsion of pride, arrogance and haughtiness, a high value being placed on humility, calmness, composure and placidity. This all translates into a reluctance to be forward, to self-promote or assert oneself in any way. Their religious services are conducted in German, and are held on a rotating basis in family homes and barns. All the accoutrements for a gathering, such as benches, dishes and food for the meal that follows a service, will often be pulled to the host's property by wagon. Pennsylvania Dutch is spoken at home and in daily discourse (a mixture of various German dialects and English), and the children learn English at school.

Singing is the only joyful expression allowed, musical instruments not being permitted in an Amish church service or at any time, as it is considered worldly and vain. However, singing is important to their lives and is always in unison and never harmonized.

Rumspringa ('running around') is the general Amish term for adolescence and the period leading up to serious courtship, during which rules may be relaxed. As in non-Amish families, this is a time when a certain amount of individual assertiveness is experienced together with a degree of misbehaviour and rebellion. This is usually overlooked though not encouraged. At the end of this period young Amish adults are expected to find a spouse and be baptized, though this must be a personal choice. At this point, some young people choose not to join the church and instead live their lives in a different community or wider society. Some communities will actively 'shun' those who decide to abandon the community, or have been disobedient in some way, having nothing more to do with them.

Everyday life and customs in the Amish community are governed by an unwritten code of behaviour called the *Ordnung*. The Ordnung governs everything from clothing and child bearing to occupational activities, and how the weekend is spent, the enforcement of these rules depending on the

Bishop, who is charged with upholding Amish values. The rules are those of togetherness and fellowship, equality, contentment, peace and love, and to worship and commune secluded from the world.

The Amish are especially known for their distinctive self-made clothing, which is essentially that of 17th century European peasants. Men and boys wear broad-brimmed black hats, dark-coloured suits, straight-cut coats without lapels, black trousers, suspenders, solid-coloured shirts and black socks and shoes. Their coats and vests are fastened with hooks and eyes as opposed to buttons. The men grow beards after they marry, but are forbidden moustaches.

The Amish women and girls wear bonnets, long full dresses with capes over the shoulders, shawls, and black shoes and stockings; their capes and aprons are fastened with straight pins or snaps. Amish women never cut their hair which is worn in a bun, and they are not allowed to wear jewellery of any kind.

Although they live in semi isolation, they are often seen making trips into their local town for groceries. They reject the use of automobiles, using bicycles or horse-drawn buggies instead. The more recent buggies are box-like in appearance and usually black, though some are white, grey or even yellow in colour, and many groups can be distinguished by their chosen colour of buggy. Earlier buggies were of less sturdy design, comprising a light, simple, two-person carriage drawn by one or two horses and having a folding top. Until the invention of the automobile, these buggies were a common means of travel, and their extensive use helped to encourage the improvement and surfacing of main roads, providing all-weather passage between towns. Nowadays, the Amish have also been seen travelling on buses, if a longer distance is called for.

The Amish are not always solemn and reserved, as they do enjoy common pastimes and games, though these are played strictly for enjoyment and not for competition. Families will often sing or read together at the end of a days' work, before retiring early.

Although the number of automobiles has now well surpassed the buggy, the Amish still use this as their transport. The term 'horse and buggy' is frequently used in reference to clinging to outworn attitudes or ideas, or outmoded, old-fashioned practices.

BUDDHISM

Buddhism is a spiritual development leading to an insight into the true nature of reality. Buddhist practices mean changing yourself in order to develop qualities of kindness, wisdom and awareness. Developed over thousands of years, the spiritual development within the Buddhist practice has created an incomparable resource for all those who wish to follow it, culminating in Enlightenment or Buddhahood. The goal, for all those who attain it, is that of ending suffering in any form.

The Buddhist philosophy does not include the idea of worshipping a creator 'god'; it is not actually seen as a religion in our Western understanding. The basics of Buddhist teaching are straightforward and practical; nothing is permanent, actions have consequences and change is possible. This being so, Buddhism addresses itself to all people irrespective of race, nationality, caste, sexuality or gender. It teaches practical methods which enable people to be fully responsible for their lives and their actions, and to realize and use its teachings in order to transform their experiences.

(Author's Note)

This code of existence I believe to be of the most valuable, in that there is nothing one could disagree with, if a life on this planet were to be a worthy one.

THE RELIGION OF ISLAM

The religion was founded by Muhammad who was born in 570 AD in a small village (Mecca) along a caravan route in what is today known as Saudi Arabia. He was interested in both Judaism and Christianity, though due to the ensuing economic security, he turned to more religious contemplation, often living in caves in the wilderness for long periods of time. Christianity at this time was about to enter the Dark Ages. He practiced fasting and was prone to dreams, receiving his first of many 'revelations' at the age of 40, thinking at that time that perhaps he was possessed by demons. He claimed that he was visited by the angel Gabriel who told him to warn the people, thus beginning his prophetic life.

The Koran (Quran) was given to Muhammad and supersedes all other revelations. To a Muslim, every word of the Koran is the Word of God and is of an eternal nature. In other words, it existed in heaven prior to being dictated by the angel Gabriel. The Koran governs every area of the life of a Muslim. They affirm that Jesus was a prophet of a previous age, and that he was born of a virgin, performing many miracles, but they vehemently deny that he was God, was crucified, or rose from the dead. The Koran allows a man to have up to four wives if he believes he can treat them equally!

The unforgivable sin to a Muslim is to attribute deity to anything other than God himself. To claim that Jesus is God or the Son of God is blasphemy to a Muslim. Muslims even refer to Muhammad as the 'Holy Spirit'. The greatest threat to world peace and stability in the next decade or two may well be the result of the religion of Islam. Almost every controversy in the Middle East can be traced to this religion, either through inter-party disagreements, or Islam versus non-Islam.

The current resurgence of Islam began with the oil cartel following the Yom Kippur War of 1973. Millions of dollars from extensive foundations are being spent to fuel the worldwide expansion of Islam, and it is the youngest of the five major religions of the world. It is estimated that there are 800,000,000 to 1 billion Muslims world-wide, with over 20 million Muslims residing in Europe. England now has over 2,000 mosques and after ethnic Russians, the Muslim population group is the largest, and growing approximately 4 times as fast. There are now 48 nations where the majority adhere to Islam. In less than 100 years Islam has spread from the Atlantic Ocean across central Asia deep into India. Having converted to Islam, hardly any countries have ever reversed their beliefs in 14 centuries of history!

'Allah' is the Arabic word for 'God', and is the sovereign Lord of the universe. Everything that occurs is according to his will, and Muslims pray five times a day facing Mecca; he is also the source of both good and evil. The Koran governs absolutely every area of the life of a Muslim, Islam being a religion of rigid monotheism and all-encompassing law, and everything is seen from an Islamic perspective. Muslims fast for one month each year during the 9th month, the lunar month of Ramadan. This month of fasting is during the day only, and is broken with feasting after sundown.

'Jihad' ('holy war') is also a religious duty of all adult males who must commit to any summons of war against infidels, and any who die in such a war are assured of paradise.

JUDAISM

The first and oldest of the three great monotheistic faiths is Judaism, the religion and life of the Jewish people. The basic tenets and laws of Judaism are derived from the Torah, the first five books of the Bible. The belief is that there is one eternal God wanting all people to behave in a just and merciful way. All people are created in the image of God, therefore deserve to be treated with dignity and respect.

Judaism does not believe that other people must follow its teachings and practices in order to reach a state of grace. The world is judged by deeds and not beliefs, everyone sharing in the future of our existence. One can convert to Judaism, though it is not a missionary religion, and any conversion has to be decided by Jewish religious authorities.

Jewish religious observance is centred mostly in the home, where daily prayers are said three times each day, the last call to prayer being at sunset. Congregational prayers take place in a synagogue, a house not only of prayer but also of study, these services being led by a cantor or rabbi, an ordained religious teacher.

Of great significance to the Jewish people is the Menorah, which has been a symbol of Judaism since ancient times, and is the emblem on the coat of arms of the modern state of Israel. In the Bible it is described as the seven-branched ancient 'lampstand' made and used in the portable sanctuary set up by Moses in the wilderness and later in the Temple in Jerusalem. There are two different types of Menorah, the seven-branched one for daily use, and a nine-branched one which is used during *Hanukkah*. Jewish followers believe that this particular symbol was designed by the Creator himself, and is said to symbolize the burning bush as seen by Moses on Mount Horeb where Moses was commanded to make a menorah that had one main 'stem' and six branches, commanding it to be placed in the 'holy place' of the Tabernacle and the Temple.

Exodus 25:31 ..... *"You shall also make a lampstand of pure gold; the lampstand shall be of hammered work. Its shaft, its branches, its bowls, its ornamental buds and flowers shall be of one piece".*

All healthy Jewish boys are circumcised on the eighth day after birth, this having been practised since the days of Abraham and is a physical sign of the Covenant. When a Jewish girl is 12 and a Jewish boy 13 they will have come of age in that they then undertake religious responsibilities. Both will then be called upon to read the Torah.

Two people identifying as Jewish may actually have different beliefs, as the religion has developed unique sects over time. The three major branches are *conservative Judaism, orthodox Judaism,* and *reformed Judaism.* These denominations obey the Hebrew Scriptures differently and so live out their faith differently. Holidays are an important event in the Jewish calendar, as they commemorate significant historical events, marking special times in the year. These include the *Sabbath, Passover, The Day of Atonement, The Festival of Booths, The Jewish New Year, The Festival of Trees* and *Purin. Hanukkah* is an important Jewish holiday commemorating an event that occurred after the sacred writings were established, being the victory of the Maccabees over the Syrian-Greek rulers of Jerusalem.

Yom Kippur is the most important and solemn of Jewish holidays, being the occasion on which otherwise non-observant Jews are most likely to attend synagogue, refrain from work, or fast. On this day not only do they obey the aforementioned but also refrain from drinking (including water) and sex. Orthodox Jews also follow the Talmudic regulations of not wearing leather shoes, not washing, and not anointing themselves with any deodorants, lotions, perfumes etc. It is traditional to wear white on this occasion, sacred clothing and garments being important to many Jews. This holiday is a happy one, as it brings about reconciliation with God and other people, and if observed properly, many people feel a deep sense of serenity by the end of the fast.

Judaism also commemorates important moments in a person's life. Regarding the young, Judaism practices *naming ceremonies,* and for boys in particular *circumcision (Brit Milah),* is an important custom, together with the wonderful celebration of the *Bar Mitzvah* when a teenager, and of course, concerning everyone, marriage.

History is of great importance to the Jewish people, as in it they see God's revelation, his work, and unfolding plan.

ABORIGINAL BELIEFS

The Australian Aboriginal belief is one of spirituality. Their beliefs are strong, believing in several spiritual entities. They believe that at the beginning of time there were creational beings who rose out of the ground in order to create the world around them, the mountains, valleys, plants and animals. This is quite similar to the Christian religion in that Christians believe God created the world and all living things in six days. The Aboriginal people refer to this period of creation as 'Dreamtime'. The time that came after this period is referred to as 'Dreaming'. Although indigenous beliefs and cultural practices vary according to region, all groups share in a common world-view that the land and other natural phenomena possess living souls. The 'Dreaming' or 'Dreamtime' is the English name given to the intimately connected but distinct strands of Aboriginal belief. They refer not to historical past but to a fusion of identity and spiritual connection with the timeless present. They express their belief in rituals of a spiritual nature, dancing, singing and painting their bodies with meaningful symbols. If, before undergoing a long journey for example, they would appeal to the creator spirit of a nearby mountain for protection, or to the spirit creator of the land on which they walked.

There were family ceremonies for puberty and entering adulthood, and fertility and burial ceremonies for friends and relatives. Some ceremonies were to ensure plentiful food for the tribe, other tribes taking part in these, if food was abundant in a particular year, sometimes travelling long distances.

Early missionaries, bent on 'saving' the Aboriginal soul, forced them to read and learn the Bible, as a result of which there are now Aboriginal people who are now Christians. However, most Aborigines still believe in the old traditional ways, though instead of believing their existence on earth to have been 'the beginning of time' they now accept that it has actually been approximately 60,000 years. Their culture is the oldest surviving culture in the world.

When the first Europeans settled in Australia in 1788 there were possibly a million Aborigines. Their population was quickly depleted through a combination of warfare, disease and dispossession of lands. One reason for the cultural acceptance of colonial violence was the mistaken belief that Aborigines had no religion, and were referred to as 'savages'.

Throughout the years they divided into large groups of different tribes which produced different cultures, and their language adapted into 250 dialects. They were nomadic people, moving through the land in cycles, sometimes meeting with, and sharing stories with, other clan-groups. It is misleading to attempt to separate Australian indigenous religious experience from other aspects of their life, culture and history. Time to them is circular, not linear, as each generation relives the Dreaming activities.

Each group has an important religious specialist who will initiate and obtain contact with spirits and divinities. Specific elders may also be keepers of specific rituals and fables. This knowledge is sometimes segregated according to gender, there being 'men's business' and 'women's business'.

The word 'Walkabout' is connected to adolescent males and their right of passage in the Aboriginal culture. 'Walkabouts' can last up to six months, and young boys walk around aimlessly with the sole purpose of connecting with the spirits. They journey through the desert, and surviving this ordeal is aided by ancestral spirits who guide them safely back home. At important stages of men and women's lives ceremonies are held to seek the assistance of spiritual beings. This directs them in the continuing process of the 'Dreaming'. Ritual ceremonies involving special sacred sites invoke these mythic and living beings and continue to provide the means to access the spiritual powers of the 'Dreaming'. The 'Dreaming' continues to this day to control the natural world. However, the continuous Christian missionary presence in Aboriginal communities since 1821 has seen many Aborigines convert to Christianity.

THE DALAI LAMA

The Dalai Lama is a Buddhist leader of religious officials of the Gelug or 'Yellow Hat' branch of Tibetan Buddhism. The name is a combination of the Mongolian word 'Dalai' meaning 'Ocean' and the Tibetan word 'Blama' meaning 'chief' or High Priest. 'Lama' is the general term referring to Tibetan Buddhist teachers. There are, however, several different translations regarding the meaning of the title, another being that of 'Ocean of Wisdom'. The current Dalai Lama is often called 'His Holiness'. Traditionally, he is thought of as the latest reincarnation of a series of spiritual leaders who have chosen to be reborn in order to enlighten others. He has indicated that the institution of the Dalai Lama may be abolished in the future, and also that the next Dalai Lama may be found outside Tibet, and also possibly female.

The title 'Dalai Lama' may also have originated from Genghis Khan when he was proclaimed emperor of a united Mongolia during 1206. He took the name Cingis Qaghan or 'Oceanic Sovereign', the Anglicized version of which is Genghis Khan.

The institution of the Dalai Lama has become a central focus of Tibetan cultural identity, and is regarded as the principal incarnation of Chenrezig, the embodiment of compassion and patron deity of Tibet. In that role the Dalai Lama has chosen to use peace and compassion in his treatment of his own people and his oppressors. In this sense he is the cornerstone of Tibetan identity and culture.

The Dalai Lamas have also functioned as the principal spiritual guide to many Himalayan kingdoms bordering Tibet, as well as western China, Mongolia and Ladakh. The writings of the Dalai Lamas over the centuries, have inspired more than fifty million people in these regions, and have become one of the world's greatest repositories of spiritual thought, reflecting the fusion of Buddhist philosophy embodied in Tibetan Buddhism.

By Himalayan tradition, upon the death of the Dalai Lama, a search for the Lama's reincarnation is conducted. Traditionally it has been the responsibility of the High Lamas of the Gelugpa Tradition and the Tibetan government. The process can take around two or three years, and the search for the 14th Dalai Lama lasted four years before he was eventually found. The search has usually been limited historically to Tibet, although the third was born in Mongolia. Tenzin Gyatso, though, has stated that there is a chance that he will not be reborn, and if he is, it will not be in the People's Republic of China. He states in his biography, *Freedom From Exile,* that after he dies it is possible that his people will no longer want a Dalai Lama, in which case there would be no search for the Lama's reincarnation. *"So I might take rebirth as an insect, or an animal – whatever would be of most value to the largest number of sentient beings".*

There are several ways in which the High Lamas can increase the chances of finding the reincarnation. High Lamas often visit the holy lake called Lhamo La-tso, in central Tibet, and watch for a sign. This might be a vision or some indication of the direction in which to search, and this was how Tenzin

Gyatso was found. The elevation and the surrounding peaks combine to give the lake an extremely changeable climate. The combination of the passage of the clouds and the direction of the wind creates a constantly moving pattern on the surface of the waters, and on that surface visions appear to those who seek them. It was here that during 1935, the Regent, Reting Rinpoche, received a clear vision of three Tibetan letters, a monastery with a jade green and gold roof, and a house with turquoise roof tiles, which led to the discovery of Tenzin Gyatso, the present 14th Dalai Lama.

Once the boy they believe to be the reincarnation has been found, he must undergo a series of tests to affirm the rebirth. He is presented with a number of artefacts, some of which belonged to the previous Dalai Lama, and if the boy chooses the items which belonged to the previous Dalai Lama, this is seen as a sign.

The boy (and his family) will then be taken by a group consisting of the three major servants of Dalai Lama, eminent officials and troops, to Lhasa, where he will then study the Buddhist sutra in preparation for assuming the role of spiritual leader of Tibet.

Many Tibetans in India felt that it was not the Dalai Lama's decision to reincarnate or not. Rather, they felt that since the Dalai Lama is a national institution, it was up to the people of Tibet to decide whether or not the Dalai Lama should reincarnate.

During September 2007 the Chinese government said that all high monks must be approved by the government, which obviously would include the selection of the next Dalai Lama. The Dalai Lama said, as early as 1969, that it was for the Tibetans to decide whether the institution of the Dalai Lama should continue, and has given reference to a possible vote occurring in the future for all Tibetan Buddhists to decide whether they wish to recognize his rebirth. The Dalai Lama has said he will not be reborn in a country controlled by the People's Republic of China or any other country which is not free.

The present 14th Dalai Lama is a revered figure around the world today, as one who represents compassion and wisdom, and always with a cheerful countenance. He has become the subject of several motion pictures, as well as documentary films.

MOTHER TERESA

This extraordinary woman was born as Agnes Gonxha Bojaxhiu on 27th August 1910 in Skopje, now the Republic of Macedonia. She considered that "poverty is a gift from God", believing and serving that motto.

Mother Teresa spent 18 years of her life in Skopje, before travelling to Ireland in 1928 to join the Institute of the Blessed Virgin Mary, sailing on later to India as a teacher.

There was some confusion with regard to her nationality and also her family, as she had never wanted to talk about them or her past. When asked questions about her nationality or her lifestyle, she answered *"I feel a citizen of Skopje, my born city, but I belong to the world"*.

As a young child she attended school in Skopje, but also attended classes at her parish. Some of these classes were taken by missionaries who recounted fascinating stories of India which inspired her curiosity and desire to leave her home town and take the long trip into the unknown, but mystically attractive India. Agnes followed the stories of the missionaries with ever-increasing interest, an interest which would make a path for her decision to serve as a missionary. Agnes, later Mother Teresa of Calcutta, never doubted that the voice of God reached to the very depths of her being.

In 1928 she became a novitiate in the Loretto Order, which ran mission schools, and took the name Sister Teresa. In 1937 she took her final vows as a nun, and after studying nursing, moved into the slums. Municipal authorities gave her the pilgrim hostel near the sacred Kali's temple where she founded her order in 1948. She adopted Indian citizenship and she, together with all her nuns, adopted the sari as their habit. In

1950 she officially founded the order Missionaries of Charity receiving canonical sanction from Pope Pius XII.

The order opened numerous centres, serving the blind, aged, cripples, lepers and the dying, and under her guidance the Missionaries of Charity built a leper colony near Asnosol in India called Shanti. While visiting India, Pope Paul VI gave her his ceremonial limousine, which she promptly raffled to help finance her leper colony.

By the late 1970's the Missionaries of Charity numbered more than 1,000 nuns who operated 60 centres in Calcutta, and more than 200 centres worldwide. By 1990, 456 centres were established in more than one hundred countries.

She said once:- *"We cannot make big things, only small, but with great love"*. Although her own life was modest, India bade her farewell at her funeral in Calcutta with spectacular ceremony.

"MIRACLES" AT LOURDES

How do we really perceive the alleged 'Miracles' at Lourdes in France?

The Grotto of Bernadette in Lourdes, France, is where a 14-year-old miller's daughter claimed to have conversed with Mary, the mother of Jesus. Mary told the girl that Catholic priests should build a chapel at this site in the foothills of the Pyrenees Mountains, where a spring would flow. This she reportedly did by digging her hands into the soil to release a stream of water that has flowed to this day. A shrine was erected together with a bath house so that pilgrims could bathe in the spring's reputed healing waters. Thousands of people began to arrive, some on stretchers and others supported by canes and crutches, which they apparently left behind to be thrown onto a huge pile for future pilgrims to marvel at. Thousands of people have reported complete cures from advanced cancers, and other serious injuries and ailments.

Out of the thousands of reported 'cures' only 66 have actually been declared 'miracles' by The Lourdes Medical Commission that evaluates each claim. However, it has been noted that many cures arise from what medical science calls spontaneous remission or regression, which supposedly takes months or years to become evident; cures that might have happened anyway, either from the body's own self-healing system, or because the disease has simply run its course.

One of these extraordinary 'miracle healings' was witnessed by a French-born American surgeon, Dr. Alexis Carrel, who a few years after this episode, would receive the 1912 Nobel Prize in Physiology and Medicine for his work on organ transplantation and blood vessel suturing. Carrel had taken up the challenge issued by a priest that he travel with the 'sick train' to Lourdes and observe what happened there firsthand, his intention being to examine the facts objectively, just as a patient is examined at a hospital or an experiment conducted in a laboratory. He confidently told medical colleagues before leaving, that whatever cures or healings that did occur at Lourdes, would be seen as a product of the incredible power of suggestion, which in itself was worthy of investigation.

Dr. Carrel witnessed an eighteen year old girl, Marie Bailly, being immersed in the women's pool, and thought her far too ill for the procedure. However, he directed that some of the water be sprinkled on her abdomen. Her legs were gravely swollen, her pulse and breathing rapid. Carrel believed she suffered from tuberculosis peritonitis. Within half an hour her breathing became less rapid, her abdomen became flatter, and by the evening she was sitting up in bed and eating. Carrel reported this inexplicable experience to the medical community in Lyons. He was then attacked on one hand by the Clergy for being sceptical, and on the other by organized medicine for being gullible.

Most instantaneous cures that have been reported and documented at Lourdes seem to involve a tremendous acceleration of the patient's own natural healing process, as though their entire self-repair and immune system had been triggered by an energetic force into a frantic drive of activity. Some of these patients reported that during their immersion in the waters of Lourdes, they instantly felt the sensation of an electrical charge or intense heat coursing through their body. Several cases of 'miraculous cures' had not even travelled to Lourdes, but had simply prayed, invoking the name of Our Lady of Lourdes.

The emotional charge that flows in some humans from their exposure to rituals, idols and ceremonies, seems to instigate their potential for self-healing. Shamans in tribal societies have known and used these techniques for thousands of years to inspire, scare, shock, or otherwise provoke their patients into an altered state of consciousness that induces their innate healing resources to function effectively.

AUTO SUGGESTION

Autosuggestion is a psychological technique that was developed by apothecary Emile Coue from the 19th century to the early 20th century. Coue graduated with a degree in pharmacology in 1876 and worked as an apothecary in Troyes from 1882 to 1910. When he began working in Troyes, he quickly discovered what later came to be known as the 'placebo effect'. He became known for reassuring his patients by praising each remedy's efficiency and leaving a small positive notice with each given medication. Coue noticed that in certain cases he could improve the efficiency of a given medicine by praising its effectiveness to the patient. He realized that those patients to whom he praised the medicine had a noticeable improvement when compared to patients to whom he said nothing.

This began the exploration into the use of hypnosis and the power of the imagination. After completing his tutelage under two leading exponents of hypnosis, Coue began relying on hypnosis to treat patients. He discovered that subjects could not be hypnotized against their will and, of more importance, the effects of hypnosis wore off when the subject regained consciousness.

He described his method as *"an instrument that we possess at birth, and with which we play unconsciously all our life, as a baby plays with its rattle. It is however a dangerous instrument; it can wound or even kill you if you handle it imprudently and unconsciously. It can on the contrary save your life when you know how to employ it consciously"*.

Although stressing that he was not primarily a 'healer' but one who taught others to heal themselves, Coue claimed to have effected organic changes through autosuggestion. He developed a method which relied on the belief that *any idea exclusively occupying the mind turns into reality,* although only to the extent that, for instance, a person without certain limbs could not possibly grow them back. However, if a person *believes* that their asthma is disappearing, this may actually happen, the body being physically able to overcome or control the illness. On the other hand, thinking negatively i.e. *"I am feeling really ill"* will encourage the body to accept this thought.

PSYCHIC SURGERY

Entering into the role of 'positive thinking', psychic surgery must surely be the ultimate. Whether you believe it or not, it certainly does exist.

Psychic surgery is a procedure involving the supposed creation of an incision using only the bare hands, the supposed removal of pathological matter, and the seemingly spontaneous healing of the incision. It has been condemned in many countries as a form of medical fraud, and a 'total hoax', also the medical profession maintains that psychic surgery may cause needless death by keeping the ill away from life-saving medical care.

It first appeared in the Spiritualist communities of the Philippines and Brazil in the mid-1900's, taking different paths in those two countries. Although psychic surgery varies by region and practitioner, it usually follows some common form. Most cases do not involve actual surgery, although some practitioners have been known to make incisions. In regions of the world where belief in evil spirits is prevalent, practitioners will sometimes produce objects, such as pieces of glass or wood, bodily tissue and clotted blood, explaining that the foreign bodies were placed in the patient's body by evil spirits.

In the Philippines, the procedure was first noticed in the 1940's, when Eleuterio Terte performed a routine 'healing'. Terte and his pupil Tony Agpaoa, who was apparently associated with *The Christian Spiritist Union of the Philippines,* trained others in this procedure.

By 1959, the procedure had come to the attention of the U.S. public, after the publication of '*Into the Strange Unknown*' by

Ron Ormond and Ormond McGill. The authors called the practice 'fourth dimensional surgery', and wrote *"we still don't know what to think; but we have motion pictures to show it wasn't the work of any normal magician, and could very well be just what the Filipinos said it was – a miracle of God performed by a fourth dimensional surgeon"*.

The origins of the practice in Brazil are rather obscure, but by the late 1950's several 'spiritual healers' were practicing in the country. They claimed to be performing their operations merely as channels for spirits of deceased medical doctors. Others were seen to be following practices and rituals known as 'Umbanda', a shamanic ritualistic religion with mediumistic overtones inherited from the African slaves brought to the country in colonial times.

Psychic surgery made U.S. tabloid headlines in March 1984 when comedian Andy Kaufman, who had recently been diagnosed with a rare lung cancer, travelled to the Philippines for a six-week course of psychic surgery. Practitioner Jun Labo claimed to have removed large cancerous tumours and Kaufman declared to believe the cancer had been removed. However, Kaufman died from renal failure as consequence of a metastatic lung cancer on May 16th, 1984.

As a result of this and several other similar cases, accusations of fraud were brought against the perpetrators. Alex Orbito, whose association with actress Shirley MacLaine was well known, was a practitioner of psychic surgery. On June 14th, 2005, Orbito was arrested by Canadian authorities and indicted for fraud, though charges were eventually dropped.

THE KNIGHTS TEMPLAR

Although Jerusalem was ultimately in Christian hands in the early 1100's, the route to the holy city was not a safe one. Christians travelling to the city encountered many skirmishes, resulting in death, from displaced Muslim infantry and highwaymen. These incidents were becoming more and more frequent.

The Muslim army in their homeland of Syria had not far to go for their supplies, and had the advantage of knowing their terrain well. The Christians' supply line, on the other hand, was not an easy one to negotiate, stretching as far as Constantinople (Turkey).

Hugh de Payen, a French knight, heard of the troubles in the holy land and set out to resolve the problem. With nine other knights he travelled to Jerusalem. These knights were landowners, though not particularly wealthy, and trained in combat. They arrived in Jerusalem with a proposition for the then king, Baldwin II, to defend Christians on their journey. Legend has it that the actual motive for the expedition was to excavate the site at Temple Mount, this being the alleged site where King Solomon had buried the Ten Commandments and other religious artefacts. The offer to defend the Christian pilgrims against attack seems rather suspect, when there were only nine knights in all, and the excavation theory appears more likely.

However, the Knights Templar were formed, and officially recognized at the Council of Troyes in 1129 with Hugh de Payen, a French nobleman, at its head. They drew up an order known as 'In Praise of the New Knighthood', outlining the rules and regulations by which the members of the order lived, this having been constructed by Bernard of Clairvaux. The full title of the order was 'The Order of the Poor Knights of Christ and the Temple of Solomon', which is now shortened to just 'Knights Templar'.

The knights vowed to live the lives of monks and therefore took vows of poverty, chastity and obedience to God. If any member broke them they were automatically expelled from the order. Over time the order grew in number and in wealth, and obtained the reputation of being 'a band of warrior monks'. It had become the object of some debate as to whether the Templars were more warrior than monk.

With regard to chastity, knights and monks in monasteries avoided women, just as nuns were kept from men, but when on crusades it was impossible to establish what each member was actually getting up to, and it was quite possible that on rare occasions a member may have broken his oath. It is also apparent that homosexuality was permitted (this is rather strange, as it is seen as a 'sin' within the Bible), with the addition of various lewd and barbaric practices incorporated in different rituals. As these 'admissions' were possibly extracted under torture, there is no actual proof as to their existence; the Templars also performed all ceremonies in the strictest of secrecy and locations,

The personal appearance and cleanliness of the Templars seems to have left a lot to be desired, according to records found in Somerset, as it states that the Templars were "arrogant, odiferous, unclean people....wearing dirty, tattered clothes....their faces burnt by the sun". They were also accused of being "abusive, proud and haughty".

According to existing records, Templars were accused of rape and adultery, which acts did not go unpunished. Nearly all those found guilty were court marshalled and expelled from the order, and some, rather mysteriously, disappearing altogether.

The Order was an extremely strict one. No-one who had been previously married could join, and no-one who was not of noble descent could join, as the Order was to be an elite group of people. All possessions such as money, land and property were all handed over to the Order so that soon the 'Poor Knights of Christ' were the richest order in Christendom, developing into a multi-branched organisation. They were the first international bankers, offering savings accounts and even loans, and in many parts of Europe, were also in charge of tithe collection on behalf of the Church. Our cheque system is derived from the Templars. As their banking system was often anonymous, monarch and peasant alike could entrust their money to the order. This bears strong resemblance to the Swiss banking system of today, and it is believed the inspiration for it came from the Templars, even speculating that the Templars themselves set up the system after fleeing to Switzerland after their dissolution. They became trustees of the bank accounts of many monarchs throughout the known world, even kings begging them for money.

They took part in major crusades led by Guy de Lusignan and Richard the Lionheart, becoming recognized as a feared enemy on the field of battle. As they attacked from horseback, most of their training was done on horses. The main weapon used by the Templars during a cavalry charge was the long lance, which over time was further developed into a shorter, more manageable size. Their sword skills were legendry, and as these weapons were extremely heavy, it took considerable strength to wield them, and they were able to cut a person in two if swung at full force.

By the 1300's the Knights Templar were the largest knightly order ever known in the history of the world, having connections with banking, taxation, property, agriculture and architecture. They had monarchs everywhere who had either invested money with them or loaned money from them. One particular monarch who had loans outstanding with the

Templars was King Philip le Bel of France. By years of war with England, Philip had inherited a country in grave financial debt and was virtually bankrupt. He saw a possible solution to the problem by approaching the then Pope Clement V, who had a reputation for being unscrupulous. Philip set about to undermine the Templars by devising a plan to expose the Order as corrupt. On the 12th October 1307, Philip sent to all police departments in France, sealed envelopes with the instruction not to be opened until the following day. On Friday 13th October, the biggest plot in history took place, and King Philip's orders were carried out. Every Templar in France was arrested and thrown into prison. This is the origin of the superstition with regard to Friday 13th.

The list of charges against the Templars was huge. They were accused of devil worship, blasphemy, sodomy, witchcraft, spitting on the cross, denying Christ and many more (the denial of Christ was one of the oaths taken on initiation, should they be taken prisoner). They were cruelly tortured, having their feet coated in fat and roasted over a slow fire. Another act of torture was to have their hands tied behind their backs and to be hung by the wrists, thus dislocating the shoulder joints. Many confessed to completely fabricated charges.

In 1312 the Order of the Knights Templar was officially dissolved. King Philip had many Templars executed and hung on public gallows so that people could see the consequences of heresy. It is rumoured that the Grand Master, Jacques de Molay (a practicing witch), muttered a curse while burning, and within the next 12 months both Clement V and King Philip IV were dead. The place where Philip's body lay was also destroyed by fire.

There are many theories surrounding the whereabouts and validity of the treasure of the Knights Templar, even to what form it takes. It could still be anywhere in Europe, even

America. The most realistic is the legend surrounding Rosslyn Chapel near Edinburgh, where it is said the 'Holy Grail' lies.

The chapel is based exactly on the original Temple of Solomon which stood on Temple Mount, and is beautifully intricate and breathtaking in design. Although it was built in the 1400's, years after the Templars were disbanded, it has a direct Templar connection. It was built by William St. Clair, a direct relative of one of the knights who appeared at the Council of Troyes in 1118, and who was rumoured to be the knight that the Temple survived through.

Approximately 10 years' ago a tapestry measuring 14 feet by 6 feet was unearthed in the Orkney Isles depicting an exact floor plan of Rosslyn Chapel, showing two antechambers guarded by the tombs of two knights. One is said to contain the Ark of the Covenant and the other the Holy Grail. The tapestry was carbon dated to the 1600's, long after the Templars ceased to exist. However, there is no actual proof that their existence conclusively died out, and for all we know, there may still be Templars operating underground today.

Henry VIII and the REFORMATION

The English Reformation began in the reign of Henry VIII, having far reaching consequences in Tudor England. After Catherine of Aragon failed to produce a male heir to the throne, Henry had no more use for her and decided that she must be got rid of. He had already decided that Anne Boleyn should be his next wife, and by 1527 Catherine was considered too old to have any more children. However, the act of marrying Anne Boleyn was not a simple issue, as Henry VIII was a Roman Catholic, and head of this church was the Pope, based in Rome.

The Roman Catholic church did not recognize, let alone support, divorce, believing in marriage for life. Husbands could not simply decide that their marriage was over, divorce and re-marry, although those who were widowed were obviously free to marry again.

If Henry went ahead and announced that as King of England he was allowing himself a divorce, he could be excommunicated by the Pope. This meant that, under Catholic Church law, your soul could never reach Heaven, a threat which the Catholic Church used to keep people under its control.

Another approach that Henry used was to make a special appeal to the Pope so that he might get special 'Papal Dispensation'. This meant that the Pope would agree to a divorce purely on the grounds that Henry was King of England, but that it would not affect the way the Catholic Church banned divorce for others. The Pope refused to grant Henry this, and by 1533 Henry's anger was such that he ordered the Archbishop of Canterbury to grant him a divorce so that he could marry Anne Boleyn. The Archbishop, not wanting to offend the King of England, granted Henry his divorce much against the wishes of the Pope.

This effectively led to England breaking away from the Roman Catholic Church based in Rome. Henry placed himself as head of the Church, and as far as he was concerned, it was all perfectly legal.

The vast bulk of the population were very angry and dissatisfied with the Roman Catholic Church and its habit of using them as a source of money. One had to pay to get married, to have a child baptised (which was essential if you wanted to get to Heaven), and there was even a charge for having to bury a friend of relative on their land (it was necessary to be buried on Holy Ground in order for your soul to get to Heaven). As a massive amount of people's money was pouring into the Catholic Church, they were not too upset at this turnabout of events, and many felt that Henry would be more lenient with regard to taking money from them. Henry, knowing of the unpopularity of the Catholic Church, used this to his advantage.

Henry VIII was made Supreme Head of the Church by an Act of Parliament in 1534. The country was ostensibly still Catholic, but the Pope's power had been ended.

The monks in England were the most wealthy Catholics, and were a threat to Henry, also being the most loyal supporters of the Pope. By the time Henry came to the throne many monks, far from helping the poor as their calling required, had grown lazy and fat, extracting money wherever possible from the villagers in their domain. Henry decided to shut down the monasteries of England – they were to disappear as though they had never been. This act was called the 'Dissolution' – they were to be dissolved!

Henry's chief minister, Thomas Cromwell, was ordered to check up on what the monks were actually doing. Anything to discredit the monks was considered useful. Not saying their prayers, not working etc., and trumped up charges were reported by Thomas Cromwell to the King, most smaller monasteries then being duly shut down. However, not all charges needed to be falsified! Monks were found to have fathered children in the village, and nuns were found to be pregnant by them. Monks were also found to be drunk at Mass.

By 1536 the smaller monasteries had mostly gone, and the larger more valuable ones by 1540, few people being sorry to see them go. Some monks were given pensions for life, but some other chief monks or abbots were hanged, though this was rare. The vast bulk of the wealth went to Henry, who used it to build defences against France on the south coast around Portsmouth.

GANDHI and Comparative Religion

India is a country where people are predominantly religious. Religion and spirituality are firmly rooted in the minds of the Indian people, being a great sustaining force, affecting all aspects of their lives. Mahatma Gandhi, having been born and brought up in India, could not escape this strong influence of religion in everything he did. The study of comparative religion was important to Gandhi, who realised that the best principle of different religions should be assimilated for the advancement of our society.

Gandhi's mission was not only to humanise religion but also to moralise it, rejecting any religious doctrine which was in conflict with morality. He therefore felt a need of the comparative study of religions to pave the way for unity and brotherhood among the followers of different religions. In the words of Gandhi, *"Is there one God for the Mussalmans and another for the Hindus, Parsis, and Christians? No, there is only one omnipresent God. He is named variously, and we remember him by the name which is most familiar to us"*. Amongst religions, other than Hinduism, no other religion inspired and impressed Gandhi more than Christianity. He was deeply influenced by the teachings of Jesus, particularly the fact that Jesus sacrificed himself for a noble cause.

Gandhi realized that true religion elevates and enlightens the inner life of human beings. According to him, the rituals, symbols, churches, temples and mosques are only aids so long as they help to nourish the inner spiritual life of their followers.

Mohandas Karamchand Gandhi was born on October 2nd, 1869 in Porbandar, India. His country had been part of the British Empire since the 18th century. Although India's civilization was one of the oldest in the world, they were nevertheless under British rule, and would remain so for most of Gandhi's lifetime. Poverty was rife in India, with dreadful overcrowding and squalor, disease and starvation, resulting in the death of thousands before the age of 35.

Gandhi's family were devout Hindus, as were most of the population. He was the youngest of six children, his father being a minor diplomat employed by the Maharajah of Porbandar. He was only eight when a bride was chosen for him, and five years' later he married the daughter of a merchant, becoming a father at the age of sixteen. However, at the age of nineteen he left his wife to take up the study of law at University College London. Being extremely interested in the religions of the world, he read the Christian Bible voraciously as well as texts of Buddhism and Islam.

In the spring of 1891 Gandhi became an official member of the British bar, and two days after passing his exam boarded a ship for India. He practiced law for some time in Bombay, though not very successfully, and later, in 1893, was offered work in South Africa. He stayed in South Africa for 21 years altogether, some of that time with his wife and family.

Like India, South Africa was part of the British Empire, and had been since the beginning of the 19th century. British settlers began immigrating in about 1820, joining the Dutch ("Boer") farmers who were already there. A social system based on race became firmly entrenched, Europeans (whites) being on one level, whilst non-whites ('coloureds', meaning Asian or half caste) were next, and at the bottom of this ranking system were the blacks.

In about 1860 Indians arrived in South Africa to work as cheap labour on the sugar plantations. After their indentured period expired (five years) they were at liberty to either return to India or remain as freelance workers. They became farmers, shopkeepers, and even entered professions such as law and medicine etc..

Gandhi built up a successful law practice and became the first 'coloured' lawyer to enter the South African Supreme Court, spending most of his time as spokesman for 'non-whites' in the country. He worked tirelessly in an effort to fight discrimination against Indians, and used non-violence as a strategy, encouraging 'peaceful' protests. However, these efforts frequently found him arrested and jailed, as were his followers.

He was always to be seen wearing simple garments of Hindu culture, a natural cotton loin cloth, shawl and sandals, showing his defiance of British rule, also bringing him closer to the people. During his time there he did achieve certain success in the area of rights for Indians, and although only a few laws were changed, there was definite improvement in their treatment.

Gandhi organized and supervised an ambulance corps during the Boer War in 1899, receiving a medal for his efforts. He again helped the government in 1906 when the Zulu Rebellion took place, but by 1914 he believed he had outlived his usefulness in South Africa, and decided to return to India to work for home rule. He had changed, and gained in confidence during his life there, and returned to his homeland having found a much stronger 'voice' with which to campaign.

In 1918 he attempted to make a point about non-violence by 'fasting' to put an end to the mistreatment of Indians, using it as a means of protest during many of his campaigns. He would simply stop eating until the opposition gave in. He did, however, allow himself sips of water. The British were well aware that if Gandhi should die, this would, in effect, make him a 'martyr', giving him even greater influence.

He became the leader of the Indian National Congress, a political party working towards self rule for India. He periodically called national strikes, and also fought British laws of censorship. Gandhi's title of 'Mahatma' (Great Soul) came about during the early 1920's, and he became the symbol of non-violent defiance of British authority, becoming well known throughout the world for his constant fight against oppression. Believing it was honourable to go to jail for a good cause, he actually spent a total of seven years in British prisons for various 'crimes against the Crown'.

When World War II broke out in 1940 Gandhi asked Britain to trade independence for India's assistance against their enemies. However, they refused and in 1942, at the age of 72, Gandhi was jailed yet again, this time for two years. The British finally agreed to a serious discussion with regard to freedom for India.

In 1947 the British Prime Minister finally announced control of India would be handed over to local authorities. The subcontinent would be partitioned, the Hindus would exist in India whilst the Moslems would inhabit Pakistan.

Riots began to break out all over India with Hindus fighting Moslems, with Gandhi urging them to 'live in peace'. He came very close to death during the last 'fast' of his life, as at the age of 78 he announced that he would not eat until both sides agreed to 'forgive and forget'. He broke his fast after six days, when leaders of the two sides at last pledged peace.

In Delhi, as Gandhi was on his way to lead prayers in the garden of Birla House, he was accosted by a man named Nathuram Godse, who was a Hindu extremist, opposing tolerance for all creeds, and who thought Gandhi had weakened the country by extending too much assistance to the Moslems. Godse fired three shots point blank at Gandhi, killing him instantly.

All over the world people mourned his passing, though he had died as he would have wished, in the service of his people. Thirteen days' later his ashes were scattered in the sacred rivers of India and into the sea off the coast of Bombay.

He died giving hope to countless fellow Indians for a better standard of living, by standing up to authority with intelligence and courage. When hatred and violence consumed millions of people, he had stood for peace, love and tolerance.

NELSON MANDELA

Nelson Rolihlahla Mandela was born in a small village in the south eastern region of South Africa known as the Transkei. His father was chief of the village and a member of the royal family of the Xhosa speaking Thembu tribe.

As a boy Mandela grew up in the company of tribal elders and chiefs, giving him a strong sense of his African heritage and self-government. He was educated in Methodist church schools, which influenced his early education. As a result of this broader way of thinking, he learned to disagree with some tribal customs, such as arranged marriages, and was later expelled from Hare University for leading a student strike.

In 1944 he joined the ANC (African National Congress), their main goal being to improve the conditions and rights for coloured people in South Africa. He worked continuously and tirelessly, instigating non-violent demonstrations against apartheid. However, these were far from successful, as they allowed the South African government to respond with violence against Africans. Although Mandela would have preferred to protest peacefully, he began to feel that non-violent resistance would have no effect, and change nothing.

The days of non-violent protest were over, and in 1961 anti-apartheid leaders created a semi-underground movement called the All-African National Action Council. Mandela was appointed its honorary secretary. Terrible massacres occurred, resulting in thousands of deaths of both blacks and whites, and in 1962 he was arrested, for the second time, on a charge of 'high treason', and was sentenced to life imprisonment on Robben Island.

During the twenty seven years Mandela spent in prison, his example of quiet dignity and suffering has made him a hero to his people, and endeared him to millions around the world. He has referred to Mahatma Gandhi as having been his inspiration in attempting to find a peaceful solution to the ever-present inhuman treatment of coloured people, and afforded Gandhi his immense admiration for the way in which he devoted his life to a similar cause.

In 1988 Mandela was hospitalized with an illness, after which his recovery was spent in less harsh surroundings. By this time, the ruling white powers within South Africa were getting desperate and international pressures for the end of apartheid were increasing. On Mandela's release from prison on the 11th February 1990 he received rapturous welcomes wherever he went around the world. He regained the presidency of the ANC, which had been given legal status again by the government. A compromise between whites and blacks was reached, and in 1991 a new democratic government gave people of all colours the right to determine their country's future.

On 27th April 1994 the first free elections, open to all South African citizens, were held. Nelson Mandela was elected president.

As president, Mandela worked vigorously to ease the dangerous political differences in his country and to build up the economy. His skill at introducing compromise, and his personal authority, helped the transition to democracy.

Mahatma Gandhi also had a strong influence on Dr. Martin Luther King, and the extraordinary movement for civil rights that he helped to lead.

Mandela, Gandhi and King were an inspiration for positive change, with an open love of mankind.

MARTIN LUTHER KING

Martin Luther King was born on 15th January 1929 in Atlanta, Georgia, in his parents' large twelve room house, in which his grandparents also lived. He first experienced racial discrimination when their white neighbours suddenly refused to let him play with their boys. As all the boys had grown up and played together for years, this was hard for him to come to terms with. In later years he and his father were asked to move to the back of a shoe shop to be fitted with shoes, away from the whites. These early incidents made a deep impression on the young boy.

He was a bright child, surpassing his peers before his first year of schooling was over. He then attended Oglethorpe Elementary School, a private school associated with Atlanta University. This was paid for by his parents at $25 a year, which covered all expenses. His teacher was Miss Lemon, who taught him that if he experienced any injustice, he could overcome it by maintaining his dignity. She encouraged her students to learn black history, and to take pride in their heritage. On later entering Booker T. Washington High School in Atlanta, although younger than most students, he nevertheless skipped some subjects, already having covered the subject matter in question.

After two years at Morehouse College, he decided that he could best serve other people by becoming a minister. He became assistant minister of the Ebenezer Baptist Church, where his father was minister, graduating from college that year at the age of 19. He went on to attend Crozer Theological Seminary in Chester, Pensylvania, and whilst there he began to study the teachings of Mahatma Gandhi. Gandhi encouraged 'passive resistance', urging people not to fight, but to stage a quiet, non-violent protest. Martin saw this method as the answer to the dreadfully unfair treatment blacks received in America.

He met his wife Coretta Scott at Boston University, whilst working on his PhD, eventually having four children, two boys and two girls. When he graduated from Boston he became minister of the Dexter Avenue Baptist Church in Montgomery Alabama. Blacks and whites were segregated in Montgomery, attending different schools, different churches etc. and sometimes blacks would be forced to stand on a bus, even though there were vacant seats in the 'white' section.

On lst December 1955, Mrs Rosa Parkes refused to give up her seat on a bus. The police were called and she was duly arrested. This action led to a revolt, literally all over America. A train porter, E.D. Nixon, bailed Rosa out of jail and started contacting others about starting a boycott on the buses, refusing to ride on them until they received fair treatment. This resulted in a very useful newspaper article, which enabled the word about the boycott to circulate.

The boycott lasted for more than a year, and the blacks walked, rode bicycles and rode in car pools to get to work, until in December of 1956 the Supreme Court ruled that bus segregation was unlawful.

In 1957 Dr. King helped to establish the Southern Christian Leadership Conference (SCLC) becoming their president. He is remembered as a prominent leader in the African American civil rights movement. Throughout his career of service King wrote and spoke frequently, drawing on his experiences as a preacher. On 14th October 1964, he became the youngest recipient of the Nobel Peace Prize, which was awarded him for leading non-violent resistance to racial prejudice in the United States.

"All I'm saying is simply that life is interrelated, that somehow we're caught in an inescapable network of mutuality, tied in a single garment of destiny. Whatever affects one directly, affects

all indirectly. For some strange reason, I can never be what I ought to be. You can never be what you ought to be, until I am what I ought to be. This is the interrelated structure of reality."
Dr. Martin Luther King

"I have a dream, that one day this nation will rise up and live out the true meaning of its creed: We hold these truths to be self-evident; that all men are created equal. I have a dream, that one day on the red hills of Georgia, the sons of former slaves, and the sons of former slaveowners, will be able to sit down together at a table of brotherhood. I have a dream, that one day even the state of Mississippi, a desert state, sweltering with the heat of injustice and oppression, will be transformed into an oasis of freedom and justice. I have a dream, that my four children will one day live in a nation where they will not be judged by the colour of their skin, but by the content of their character. I have a dream today." Dr. Martin Luther King

At 6.0 a.m. on 4th April 1968, a shot rang out. Dr. Martin Luther King, who had been standing on the balcony of his room at the Lorraine Motel in Memphis, now lay sprawled on the balcony floor, a gaping wound now covering a large portion of his jaw and neck. A great man who had devoted thirteen years of his life to dedicating himself to non-violent protest, had been assassinated by a sniper's bullet.

As a result of this outrage, many blacks took to the streets across the country in a massive wave of riots. The FBI investigated the crime, though many believed them to be partially or fully responsible for the assassination. A man was arrested, but many people thought him to be innocent, including Martin's own family.

Martin Luther King was a charismatic man of vision and determination, and as a Baptist minister, was a moral leader to the community.

AKHENATEN, NEFERTITI and the ARMANA Period

We actually know very little about Akhenaten the man, but he has been an endless fascination with regard to his very courageous attempts to change the religion of Egypt.

Akhenaten came to the throne of Egypt in approximately 1353 BC after the reign of his father Amenhotep III. Amenhotep's reign had been a prosperous one where diplomacy seems to have replaced the relentless military campaigning of his predecessors. The end of his reign culminated in magnificent celebrations in Thebes (Luxor), the religious capital of Egypt, and home to the state god Amun-Re.

The new king was crowned as Amenhotep IV, and the construction of various temples, plus decoration projects began, portraying the new king in all his glory. However, it was not long before a radical change was seen to be happening. The art of his predecessors was to be seen in his earliest work, but within a very short time he was building temples to the Aten, or divinised sun-disk at Karnak in a very different artistic style. At this point he changed his name to Akhenaten in honour of the newly created Sun God.

Akhenaten's wife was the renowned beauty Nefertiti, who had artistic ideas of her own. She was also known for her use of cosmetics such as scents and perfumed oils, all in beautifully carved bottles. Other aids to beauty such as curlers, tweezers, razors and kohl (eye-shadow) were also used. The use of these cosmetics goes back far in Egyptian history; for example, rescued from the robbed and ransacked grave of Queen Hetephers (of the Old Kingdom) were her gold razors. Nefertiti brought back the fashions of dress from this period, tight-fitting and clinging.

She ruled alongside Akhenaten during the eighteenth dynasty from 1550-1292 BC. Her name means 'the beautiful one has arrived'. Nothing much is known about her ancestry, and no evidence has yielded information regarding her immediate family. It is thought that she might have been the daughter of Aye due to inscriptions found inside his tomb which proclaimed him the father of her sister Mutnodjmet.

Her reign with Akhenaten was unlike those of a traditional Egyptian queen. She was much more than just a typical queen in that she was a constant source of support to her husband, helping to promote his views. During her reign Egypt went through many radical religious changes. After literally hundreds of years of traditional culture and worship, a whole new concept was introduced – Monotheism. She and her husband are most famous for bringing order and discipline to the Egyptian religion, grouping all cults as manifestations of and subsidiary to one major deity, the Sun Aten. They built their 'new' religion on a solid, traditional base, and it was more a matter of ordering things, systematising them differently, neatening up the enormous polytheism of Egyptian beliefs and rituals, than of taking a new radical step. It has always amazed Egyptologists that there was no rebellion against the change from the priests of Amon (who had held the highest positions before for 1000 years – and would do so again after Nefertiti's death).

Akhenaten set about shutting down the temples; old gods were disregarded and priests were forced to change their ways to a modern and totally different way of worship. Nefertiti changed her name to Neferneferuaten-Nefertiti meaning 'the Aten is radiant of radiance because the beautiful one has come'. She took on powerful roles that in the past only Egyptian kings had carried out. She was quite often depicted with the crown of a pharaoh, or in scenes of battle smiting her enemies.

Some Egyptologists believe that perhaps Akhenaten was born with certain deformities, judging by his rather extraordinary shape when depicted on walls, tablets, columns etc., though the new form of art that he introduced portrayed people in a slightly elongated and disproportionate style. He is said to have had poor eyesight, also possibly arthritis, thus perhaps relying on his wife Nefertiti to carry out more than her required number of duties.

In the past, the Egyptians had worshipped a whole array of gods who were represented in human or animal form, or as animal-headed humans, and from early periods solar gods such as the sun god Re had already played an important role in their religion, connecting the power of the sun to the power of the Pharaoh. With the arrival of this new religion, solar gods again became prominent, among them the Aten, the visible sun-disk they could see traversing the sky each day. Akhenaten elevated the Aten to the position of 'sole god', this being portrayed as a disk with rays of light terminating in hands which reached out to the royal family. Everywhere Akhenaten and his family are shown worshipping the Aten or simply indulging in everyday activities beneath the disk.

The change in art form was to be seen in the colossi and wall-reliefs from the Karnak Aten Temple. The highly exaggerated and quite grotesque forms were very different from the formality and restraint with which Egyptian royal families and the elite had expressed themselves in the past. Although we view these forms as strangely beautiful today, in Akhenaten's reign they must have appeared quite shocking to the populace of that time. However, Nefertiti gave high status to artists, and a most beautiful new flowing style appears in the murals at Amarna, the royal seat of government. The elegance of the ancient Egyptians was not only reflected in their surroundings but also in their personal 'toilets'. They were immaculately well groomed and personally fastidious.

Although Akhenaten and Nefertiti had six daughters, there were also other wives, including the enigmatic Kiya, who may have been Tutankhamun's mother. The love that this family had for each other is beautifully portrayed in the wall murals created at the time of their reign. In Armana the King and Queen are shown everywhere together, eating, drinking, talking, planning, giving gifts, worshipping and riding together in the chariot. At the pageant of the Gathering of the Tribute, Nefertiti has her right arm round the King's waist, her left hand in his, as they sit enthroned, and the most touching scene that has been found in Egypt is one of her and her husband grieving at the death of their daughter Maketaten.

Akhenaten and Nefertiti were quite insular, in that they did not travel around as Pharaohs usually did, but stayed in their home-base at Amarna, leaving their officials to govern by 'presence' elsewhere.

Akhenaten died in his seventeenth year of reign, leaving his co-regent Smenkhkare to continue in his place. However, Smenkhkare did not remain in power for long, as the throne passed to the then very young Tutankhamun (originally Tutankhaten), who was most likely the son of Akhenaten and Kiya. During the early part of Tutankhamun's reign the regents administering the country on his behalf soon abandoned the city of Armana and the worship of the Aten and returned to Egypt's traditional gods and religious centres. The people shut up their houses and returned to the old capitals at Thebes and Memphis, reinstating the temples and cults of the gods of old.

During the process of returning to their traditional cults, a whole-scale obliteration of all things associated with Akhenaten took place. His image and names were removed from monuments and his temples were dismantled. The stone from these was reused in the foundations of other more orthodox royal buildings. The desert gradually claimed the city of Armana, reducing its buildings to little more than rubble.

Akhenaten's name and those of his immediate family were omitted from official king-lists so that, until archaeological discoveries at Armana, they were virtually unknown. Recent discoveries have made Akhenaten, Nefertiti and Tutankhamun the most famous of all rulers of ancient Egypt.

THE DANGER OF 'CULTS'

In 1978 the 'Reverend' Jim Jones of California led his followers into an isolated South American village supposedly away from the pressures of the twentieth century and his conviction of an approaching 'apocalypse', or dramatic end to the world. Everyone inside this community believed they were being persecuted by outside enemies, and this desperate feeling of persecution led them to be persuaded by Jones to end their lives. The mass suicide of nine hundred men, women and children in a Guyanan jungle brought home to many the dreadful danger of religious fanaticism.

Another mass suicide occurred fifteen years' later in 1993, in Waco, Texas, with another leader making similar prophecies. His followers retreated into a heavily defended compound where they stockpiled food and ammunition sufficient to withstand an armed, military attack. They viewed anyone outside their community as evil and a threat to their way of life. However, law enforcement officers brought about siege conditions which eventually resulted in a holocaust, killing virtually all who were left in the compound.

There have been mass cult suicides since then in Canada and Switzerland by members of the 'Solar Temple Cult'. Another group in California believed that a passing comet had come to take them to a better world. Thirty-nine young people took their own lives believing they were servants of a 'Higher Source'. When their bodies were found they were all identically dressed and lying neatly in rows.

The leader of a group is usually a very charismatic and dominant personality, and members are gradually alienated from the rest of society; in some cases being totally removed from it, living completely detached from normal life. Some ways in which this isolation is achieved are extremely worrying. The recruits are 'brainwashed' into accepting the word of their leader who effectively removes any attachment to family or friends. They are never left alone for long periods to recover their thoughts and feelings, but are subjected to incessant meetings which deprive them of sleep, and any natural resistance is destroyed.

Once having been accepted into the group, in effect it is impossible to leave. Psychological pressure, and sometimes physical force, is used to dissuade the person from leaving and to change his or her mind. All outside influences, such as parents or friends, are described as enemies and actually to leave the group is seen to be an attack on the leader.

Gradually members are conditioned into not thinking for themselves and are encouraged to accept without question the word of the leader, his decisions and his teachings. A large part of the repertoire consists of chanting and singing, they are also given a diet that is nutritionally inadequate, allowing them to become more susceptible to suggestion. Another very sinister way of controlling individuals in the group is the use of drugs.

Members are persuaded to hand over all personal wealth to the group and, as they are told that all their needs will be catered for, their desire for material things will be nonexistent. In effect, these people are totally lost to the outside world, denouncing anything remotely connected to it.

OPUS DEI

Opus Dei or *'The Work of God'*, operates essentially as a dangerous, wealthy, powerful and mind-controlling cult, embedded in the heart of the Roman Catholic Church. It seeks new recruits throughout the Church using a number of sophisticated and highly developed psychological mind-controlling techniques. It intrudes into the most intimate areas of member's lives, encouraging them to inform on each other, and drains their financial resources. Members are not allowed to disclose their allegiance.

Opus Dei is one of the most controversial movements within the Roman Catholic Church, and is said to be supported by various Popes and conservative Catholic leaders. Both Pope John Paul II and Pope Benedict XVI have been vocal support-ers of the organization.

Opus Dei was founded in Spain in 1928 by Josemaria Escriva de Balaguer, and the stated aim of the organization is to *"spread throughout society a profound awareness of the universal call to holiness through one's professional work, carried out with freedom and personal responsibility"*. Opus Dei is made up of lay members and priests who continue their work in the secular world, but remain under the strict spiritual direction of Opus Dei. All their members follow *'the plan for life'* made up of spiritual practices such as daily Mass, rosary, spiritual reading and mental prayer, as well as Opus Dei prayers and customs. Members pledge to remain celibate, and in general live in Opus Dei houses. They commit their entire salaries to Opus Dei, submitting incoming and outgoing mail to their directors. They are known to practice various forms of corporal mortification, including use of the '*cilice*', a spiked chain worn around the thigh, and use of the '*discipline*', a knotted rope for whipping.

Despite its seemingly noble intentions, the organization has stirred up controversy in countries around the world, for the way in which it operates. Opus Dei has stated that there are approximately 80,000 members worldwide, located in many countries, including Spain, Italy, Canada, Mexico, Japan, Australia, the Philippines, countries in Central and South America, the United States, Ireland and England and many others.

They are known to establish centres in or near prestigious universities etc. where they hope to attract recruits. Sadly, most Opus Dei members do not realize that the ideals they aspire to do not correlate with their actual practices, which include a culture which demands aggressive recruiting, the withholding of information, blind obedience to superiors and intense coercion and guilt on those who wish to make free decisions.

THE OUIJA BOARD

Communicating with the dead through spirit mediums swept Europe and the United States during the latter part of the 19th century. Seances were held, in which people sat around a small table, asking the board questions to which the board would answer. The 'spirits' made themselves known by either tipping the table or tapping on the floor with its legs. The taps were then interpreted by the medium for her guests.

Capitalizing on the craze for spiritualism, the mediums did not hesitate to suggest that the Ouija was definitely a portal to the spirit world, to relatives and friends of all ages.

The name 'Ouija' comes from the French and German words for yes, 'oui' and 'ja'. There are several types of Ouija Boards, which have differing layouts and can be made from a variety of materials. The board consists of the letters of the alphabet, numbers from 0-9, the words 'Yes' and 'No', and with sometimes the addition of 'Goodbye'. The board can form a rectangle or a circle and comes with a 'planchette', a device, mostly heart-shaped with a hole in the centre, that is said to move of its own free will whilst the participants' fingers are lightly placed over it. The spirits 'speak' by moving the planchette to spell out a message, or the answer to a question, on the board.

The Ouija Board has inspired its own body of superstitions and legends. Most of these superstitions concern making sure that evil spirits cannot interfere and create mischief or possibly worse. Strange, and ultimately 'evil', things have been known to happen, subsequently the board is treated with considerable respect.

I have my own story with regard to the use of the Ouija board. My mother, Marjorie Leslie, sailed home to Calcutta aboard the 'Kaiser-i-Hind' after leaving her boarding school in England, in 1920. She had been born in Calcutta, along with her brothers and sister Helen, the family presence in India having originated from missionaries who settled in the early 19th century.

Whilst experiencing extreme boredom one day during the monsoon season she, together with her sister Helen and my grandmother, decided it might be fun to have a go at finding out the whereabouts of their brother Andrew by using the Ouija board. Apparently he was due to arrive home, but had not yet put in an appearance. They asked the board *"Where is Andrew?"*. With their hands on the planchette, they waited. Suddenly it began to move quite rapidly over the board, darting quickly from one letter to the next. It spelt out "CASS". They all thought this was rather odd, as they could not connect anything or anybody with what had just appeared, and put the board away as being rather a waste of time. However, two days' later Andrew arrived home with his new fiancé CASSANDRA! This was the very first time they had either seen or met her, or known anything about her. They were all totally shocked, and my grandmother forbade the use of the board in future, all of them acknowledging that this was not a 'game' and, as they had just witnessed, was not to be taken lightly.

THE HISTORY OF DOWSING

Dowsing has been used for nearly 7,000 years, possibly longer, for finding water, gold, metals, people, animals and also to foretell the future and conjure up the past. In the middle ages it was used to find coal and water, and was used by both the Chinese and the Egyptians for thousands of years. Present day dowsing is used for archaeological and geological work, and also to locate damaged pipes and cables.

The traditional tool used for dowsing is a forked wooden rod, such as hazel, willow, ash and rowan. The dowser holds the forked end of the rod with the palms of the hands turned upwards. When the rod moves over water, metal etc. it will tremble and dip down marking the spot. The explanation given by the dowser for this phenomenon is that the corpuscles rising from springs or minerals, entering the rod, force it to bow down, in order to render it parallel to the vertical lines that the effluvia created as they rose. In effect, the mineral or water particles were supposed to be emitted by means of subterraneous heat, or of the fermentations in the interior thereof. As the rod was of light, porous wood, it gave an easy passage to those particles.

The technique spread to England with German miners who came to England to work in the coal mines. During the Vietnam War, some U.S. Marines have been known to use dowsing to locate weapons and tunnels.

Expert dowsers are allegedly capable of measuring blood toxicity, white cells, sugar levels, and detecting human illness and health.

THE WORSHIP OF WATER

Ancient Greeks worshipped rivers, streams, wells, springs, and other bodies of water for their divination properties. They performed many sacrifices and rituals to the river gods, and each river had its own priest. A bowl of water was often used in the ritual of casting spells and was an important component of magical practice.

Mother Earth was a very important figure in ancient Greek religion, as they believed that she sent the streams and her son Archeloos, who was known as the river god, to the earth. They believed that, because the rivers travelled underground, they were thought to have divine power, and as they could disappear underground then reappear above ground, the rivers were believed to be gates to the underworld. Holy wells were connected with heroes and the dead, which were both thought to reveal the future to the living.

Along with divination rituals with bodies of water, a vessel of water was frequently used as an instrument, the practice being called 'lekanomancy'. The ritual involved using a cup or bowl of water from a Holy well. Objects were then thrown into it and where they rested was used to foretell the future.

Also noted are accounts of ancient Greeks placing a mirror in the Holy Springs at the Sanctuary of Demeter at Patrai as a mode of divination. After praying, they looked into the mirror to uncover the future that the reflection revealed. Mirrors were also used as a tool for water divination.

THE HISTORY OF TAROT

The Tarot deck is a pack of beautifully painted cards, and one of the most ancient and symbolic of the many mystical future-telling arts. They appeared in Western Europe in the late Middle Ages around the onset of the Renaissance. Many enlightened mystics used and adapted the Tarot deck, creating their own designs, these being the embodiment of much symbolism and history.

The exact origin of the Tarot is not clear. It is possible that they may have originated from a card game in the sixth century in the Middle East. The Tarot deck is actually two decks mixed together, the Major Arcana and the Minor Arcana, and although they have separate origins, similar symbolism runs through both decks; they are not kept separately, but as a single pack. The gypsies are credited with bringing them to Western Europe in the fourteenth century as they wandered, and in more recent years, soldiers also spread the cards on returning from wars. The gypsies are thought to have used fairly modern seventy-eight and eighty-four card decks as early as the twelfth century, and it seems unlikely that the decks could have been combined earlier.

As they grew in popularity in Western Europe, they were adapted by many different artists and mystics, however the symbolism remained constant throughout many interpretations, soothsayers adding their own messages in symbols through the ages. These symbols and their meanings are still constant in decks today.

The highly religious life of Medieval people greatly influenced the design of the cards, religion being firmly intertwined with the symbolism of the Tarot deck, their meaning quite clear. It was not considered blasphemous to use the Tarot deck for games, and most decks were actually used for games as much as they were used for readings.

Tarot cards were banned in 1463, as a result of pressure from the clergy, although many decks were smuggled into England, and in the rest of Europe mystics continued to use the decks unhindered.

Mystics declare that the cards must be handled carefully to prevent damage and retain their accuracy; they should be wrapped in silk and kept in a wooden or silver box, and should not be passed around for use by other people, as this would destroy the reader's 'aura'.

ALEISTER CROWLEY and the Thoth Tarot

Aleister Crowley believed that he was the greatest of the world's magicians brought back to life. He was generally misunderstood and even feared during his lifetime with regard to his brilliance being channelled into the 'black arts'.

He was born in October, 1875 in Warwickshire, England, the son of a brewer and part-time preacher in the church of the Plymouth Brethren, whose enthusiasm for his religion being the only true form of Christianity, prompted him to train young Aleister to preach alongside him from an early age. When the boy rebelled, his mother reacted by dubbing him 'the beast', implying that her son's rejection of their faith was somehow motivated by the devil. Aleister took this implication very much to heart; this began a fascination with non-Christian religions and the black arts.

In an era noted for decadence and religious experimentation and deviation from the rigid Christian doctrines suffocating the Victorian society, he diverged from the more bizarre religious factions into satisfying his insatiable lust for sensation. He began a lifelong study of the occult, and his thirst for knowledge would lead him to travel all over the world, studying the Eastern mystics and the pagan religions of an ancient civilization.

When he believed he had reached the height of spiritual awareness, he wrote his 'The Book of Law'. This was a three-part poem, proving extremely influential among fellow occultists. It maintained that the age of Horus was upon mankind, ushering in the age of 'Thelema', a Greek word meaning 'will'. The central theme of 'The Book of Law' is 'Do what thou wilt shall be the whole of the law'. Although some have interpreted this to justify a life of self-indulgence, Crowley placed a different interpretation on his words, seeing in the world 'will' the ability to control the actions of others or create a change in one's surroundings through one's psychic abilities. He determined to dedicate the remainder of his life to developing his Thelemic philosophy, concentrating on this development of will, which was referred to by him as 'magic'. The Satanic number 666 became extremely important in his teachings, and he began to call himself 'The Great Beast'. This name provoked a reputation for wickedness among most people, which only added to his growing sense of self-esteem and empowerment.

As a young man, Crowley attended Trinity College, Cambridge, where he wrote poetry, publishing his first book 'Aceldama, a Place to Bury Strangers In'. He left before receiving his degree, his academic pursuits not really holding his interest, opting instead to devoting himself to mastery of the occult.

He joined the London chapter of the Golden Dawn, the first order of the secret Great White Brotherhood of Rosicrucians. The Order included elements of astrology, the tarot, alchemy, and magic. Crowley dubbed himself 'Count Vladimir' and began moving up through each successive level of ability. He graduated from the first order and sought entry into the second. However, after his advancement was thwarted through jealousy of his position, he was attacked by several henchmen. He decided to leave England to travel and study independently.

In 1906 Crowley founded his own chapter of the order of the Great White Brotherhood, known as the Astron Argon or Silver Star. Four years' later he joined a German cult of Freemasons called the Ordo Templi Orientis (OTO). They too were deeply involved in magic, and he eventually became the head of the Order. He restricted the OTO to conform to his Thelemic principles, and broke with the Freemasons, thereafter allowing men and women to join.

As Crowley gained in power, he also gained in notoriety, and in 1923 he was exiled from Cefalu, Sicily, where he had formed a branch temple, after a scandal immerged involving several prostitutes. Taking the event in his stride, he merely bragged that he had been 'expelled from Italy'. The rumours grew with regard to his leadership of rituals involving the celebration of the Black Mass, animal sacrifice, hallucinogenic drugs, and debauched sexual practices. Carrying on these practices undeterred, he published several books during the 1920's, namely *'Confessions'*, *'The Herb Dangerous'*, *'The Winged Beetle'* and *'Clouds Without Water'*. Adding fuel to his reputation as a Satanist, he carelessly remarked in an essay that "for nearly all purposes, human sacrifice is best". These comments, when made public, did nothing to endear him to society, though he continued to attract a small but loyal band of converts.

In 1937 Crowley was keen to develop his *Thoth Tarot* , and was introduced to Lady Frieda Harris, a talented artist, whom he possibly met through Masonic links. Frieda Harris was married to Percy Harris who served as an MP, and was Chief Whip for the Liberal Party. Her husband was created a baronet in 1932, therefore she was able to style herself 'Lady Harris'.

The deck was originally meant to be traditional, but Harris encouraged Crowley to commit his occult, magical, spiritual and scientific knowledge to the project. She also used her society contacts to find financial backers for the exhibition of the paintings, the catalogues, and the publication of the Tarot deck. Throughout the project she insisted on her own anonymity, though she revelled in working for such a notorious man. The finished deck was the most beautifully designed and orchestrated work of art, and one that is the most popular with followers of the occult today, the paintings having a geometric yet ethereal quality. The *'Book of Thoth'* was then published in a 200 copy limited edition, but neither Crowley nor Harris lived to see the deck itself printed.

By the mid 1930's, reality caught up with Aleister Crowley. His lavish lifestyle had extended far beyond his thirty thousand pound inheritance, and a heavy drug addiction did little to stabilize his financial position. By 1939 Crowley's creditors were forced to take a small percentage of the money owed following bankruptcy proceedings. He continued to support himself through royalties from published books such as *'Diary of a Drug Fiend'*, *'The Book of Thoth'*, and *'Magic in Theory and Practice'*. His home had been reduced from his elegant lodgings in Jermyn Street, Piccadilly, to a room in a boarding house.

He shocked and alienated even more people by commenting that *"Before Hitler was, I am"*. The backlash from this comment reduced him to a pathetic, jealous and disturbed man. He died in Hastings, England, on December 1st, 1947, at the age of seventy-two, after his physician had refused to supply the morphine on which Crowley had become addicted.

FOOD FOR THOUGHT (Cont'd)

To be able to *trust* in a belief, to be able to *be convinced* that you are right, is reassurance in itself. There is no doubt that religion has helped individuals. For some, singing and 'praying' in church seems to be the only way in which we reach the inner recesses of our souls; the only opportunity to be in tune with ourselves. This I believe to be the reason some of us keep going back, in recognition of our spiritual side, and who we *really* are. Unless we are in the habit of meditating, this would be the one and only occasion we give ourselves the time to actually *feel* , and to tap into a dimension hitherto seldom explored; a primeval connection to the ethereal, inherent but dormant in our earthly capacity. This act of blind faith, however, has guided many a person through enormous stress. *How do we replace this? If the whole concept is mythical and not proven, how do we overcome this?*

Those sceptics who think that when our life ends we, as grounded mortals, are no more, are surely not allowing themselves to see beyond, recognizing the invisible spirit – the driving force that makes us individual, unique. This tenuous thread lives on without the encumbrance of terrestrial form.

We *need* spirituality. We are spiritual beings, connected to the universe by an invisible umbilical cord – all one, all of us connecting with each other. Religion, far from uniting, separates. We all, within our designated religions, believe that our 'way' is the only true path, a guarantee of safe acceptance into paradise. We view others of a different doctrine with some scepticism, thinking perhaps that really their beliefs are fanciful, not portraying the 'true' message.

We are *afraid* to lose our faith, our religion, for if we did there would be no rudder to steer us, no anchor to stabilise us and, in some cases, no meaning to life itself. For lonely individuals the church offers a bustling social life, acceptance into a hallowed circle, and brings purpose to their existence. The priest or vicar becomes the pivotal figure in their lives, and for those of a devout (or obsessional) nature the church becomes the hub of everyday existence, taking on special significance within the boundaries of its religious teachings. They feel *safe*, secure in the knowledge that, if anything untoward should happen, they would feel the one person they could turn to would be their priest or vicar, their character being without blemish. How we could all have been duped into believing in this form of brainwashing is quite fascinating, and to have it passed down from generation to generation, without question, even amazing. You would think, with the curiosity of youth, that someone would have challenged their parents openly, asking for a valid explanation, the fairytale being just too much to actually swallow, though I suppose with hindsight, we respected our parents enough to take for granted that they knew best. However, the calling to account of religion, and the aura of mystique that surrounds it, has not seen the light of day in any recognizable capacity, until now. There will be those who do not *want* to listen, as their world would, in effect, be turned upside down should their belief be challenged, and their very existence brought into question.

I am certainly not saying that all religious leaders are corrupt. Although there are many who genuinely care for mankind and help in any way they can, in our Christian and Western world, their faith in the Bible remains absolute.

The message is of unity, love and respect, living in the knowledge that there is a power greater than ourselves; a spiritual being if you like, a force, an energy uniting each one to the other. If we 'tune in' to each other we can tell what the other is thinking. We can 'sense' when someone else comes up behind us or enters a room, without actually seeing them. We can detect when we are being threatened or when there appears to be a certain 'atmosphere' in a room, be it occupied or empty. We can also *feel* someone looking at us from a distance without visual affirmation.

There is definitely *power* in positive thinking – the 'power of prayer' is often quoted as having a remarkable impact. This I believe to be collective *thought* having a truly astonishing effect sometimes, the power of several minds concentrating on a single concept and producing a quite spectacular result.

It is a source of comfort to most of us to believe there is 'someone' or 'something' greater than ourselves to which we reach out in times of trouble or stress, knowing that we are not alone. To be entirely alone in the universe is a very frightening feeling, when it appears there is absolutely no-one to whom we can turn for help and guidance.

I believe that Christianity, as we know it, will definitely be put under a microscope in the future, and will be found wanting. Much as some of us desperately want to believe in the original '*Christmas Story*' and the '*Resurrection of Christ*', in view of scientific evidence, these 2000-year-old parables will be challenged and the very essence of Christianity brought into question.

All this might seem ironic in view of the fact that I come from a very devout Christian family, my ancestors having been missionaries in India.

The following are examples of courageous endeavour to bring 'God's word' to the native population of India, and my own family's involvement with the Christian Religion and the founding of Missions there.

WILLIAM BAWN ADDIS

My great-great-uncle William Bawn Addis studied at the Mission College in London and was appointed by the London Missionary Society to be a *Teacher of Christianity* at the port of Quilon on India's southwest coast.

The Addis family's life in India began when William sailed to South India on 10th April 1827 on the ship *'George'* to be a Christian Teacher under the auspices of the London Missionary Society. To do this, he had the necessary permission of the United Company of Merchants of England Trading to the East Indies (later called the British East India Company) to reside in South India.

He arrived at the port of Madras, in southeast India, on 5th August 1827. Here he met Susanna Emilia van Someren, whom he married only months after his arrival on 22nd November 1827, in the Madras Presidency. In 1828 he was ordained at Nagercoil, and was instructed to start a new Mission Station at Coimbatore.

Susanna Emilia van Someren was a woman particularly suited to a marriage of Missionary inclination. She was the daughter of European parents, Jamericus van Someren and Susanna Emilia Lightburne, but had been born in India, and so was able to speak the local vernacular form of the Tamil language and was familiar with local customs. She also had another advantage for William. She had been orphaned early in life, and at the age of seven had been adopted into the family of the Rev. Dr. Adoniram Judson, a well known American Baptist Missionary of the celebrated *Burmah Mission*. He encouraged her enthusiasm for mission work, and helped train her for it. Judson's wife, Ann Hasseltine Judson, was reputedly the first American woman Missionary, and she must also have had an influence on young Susanna during her seven years in the Judson household.

In 1830 William arrived at Coimbatore with his wife Susanna and their first two children. This was to be the first Protestant Mission in a province of about one and a quarter million people, mainly on the coastal plain about 900 feet above sea level, but with Coimbatore itself at 1500 feet and with a population of about 40,000.

Northwards from the town the ground rises into hill country around the hill stations of Coonoor and Ootacamund (known as Ooty) and the surrounding Nilgiri Hills.

William visited other places in the district furthering the course of his work of forming new churches and establishing schools. He remained based at Coimbatore for the rest of his working life, until ill health of both William and his eldest son forced their retirement from the Mission in 1861. All through this thirty-year period William had been assisted in his work by both his wife Susanna and his eldest son Charles, who from 1850 was also employed by the London Missionary Society as an Assistant Missionary at Coimbatore.

In retirement at Coonoor, William wrote a book on his years at the Coimbatore Mission, though declined to put his name to the work as he saw it more as a record of God's work than of his family's lives.

After William's death Susanna continued to live at Coonoor and died there aged almost ninety. She was buried at All Saints Church, Coonoor close to her husband.

William's eldest son, Charles, followed in his father's footsteps working at Coimbatore as an Assistant Missionary. Despite suffering from problems of epilepsy he managed to continue his work at the Mission, but never married.

ANDREW LESLIE

My great-great-grandfather, Andrew Leslie, also became a Missionary in India. In 1818, at the age of twenty, he began four and a half years of theological study at the Baptist Mission Academy in Bristol, during which time he met and married Eliza Franklin, the daughter of the Reverend Francis Franklin of Coventry.

The Franklin family were devout Baptists with strong and passionate religious beliefs which were instilled into Eliza and her sisters, who ran the Franklin School for Gentlewomen in Warwick Row.

On completion of his studies, Andrew was ordained at Coventry in 1823 and sixteen days later he and Eliza left for India to join William Carey's Baptist Mission movement based at Serampore. After some time at the Serampore Mission, they travelled along the Ganges to the mission station at Monghyr. However, it seems that Eliza's health was not sufficiently robust to counter the conditions of India and she died, at the age of twenty, from cholera. Andrew stayed on, travelling up and down the Ganges to Dinapur, Patna, Hajipor as well as Purneah, Tirhool, Bhaugulpore, Seetakund, Rajpore and Sultangunge. The following passage, from a memoir of Andrew Leslie, gives some indication of the sacrifices he was prepared to make in order to "spread the word of God":-

"A common car is hired – the article is as rude as it can be, and is drawn by two bullocks attended by their owner or his servants. On this vehicle the Missionary puts a small tent, a light cot in which to sleep, a box of gospels, tracts etc. another box containing kettles, a seat, and a few other things, such as he may require. But as he rarely goes without being accompanied by one or more Native Christians, their bedding, cooking

utensils, and food, are also put on the cart. The whole being ready, away they start, walking alongside the bullocks. As they proceed, as many of the villages as possible are entered into, the inhabitants called together, addressed, and books given to those who can read. When night comes on, the cart is stopped, the tent is taken off and erected, the bullocks fed and tied up under an adjoining tree, the supper of the company is eaten, worship in the native language is performed, conversations held with the villagers, who usually come out to see the travellers, and when all is over, Natives and Europeans creep into their little gypsy tents to sleep, as well as the mosquitoes with their bites and the jackals with their howlings, will allow them. As for dinner, that is generally out of the question; indeed, it not infrequently happens that the Missionary does not see or taste animal food during the whole of his journey, his only subsistence being rice, tea bread and salt butter, and a little fruit now and then. In this way some Missionaries have been known to walk several hundred miles in the course of one cold season; and it not infrequently happens that during the whole of this period, the Missionary never sees a white face, nor hears a word of his native language."

It has been recorded that Andrew Leslie had considerable influence in encouraging one Lieutenant Henry Havelock in the founding of army chaplaincy. Havelock was unable to reconcile the concept of preaching religious faith with that of killing, albeit in the line of duty. Reportedly, Andrew asked Havelock why he wouldn't preach. Havelock questioned if it would be right for him to preach, to which Andrew affirmed *"Certainly"*.

Havelock became famous for his energetic preaching and was later to rise to world fame in the Indian Mutiny of 1857, when as General of the 13th Regiment of Native Infantry, he relieved Lucknow from the Indian uprising.

In 1833, seven years after Eliza's death, Andrew married Mary Ann Chamberlain, whom Eliza had tutored when they first arrived. In December 1835 they had a son, Sheppard John, who in years to come became my mother's (Marjorie Leslie's) grandfather.

Following their marriage, Andrew and Mary Ann continued with their missionary work. Mary Ann wrote:-

"Mr. Leslie is lawyer, doctor, judge and parson. He makes wills, buries and arbitrates."

One of his deeds as a doctor had interesting results. After accidentally curing a woman of insanity by the use of a powerful snakebite remedy it was quoted that:-

"Mr Leslie is looked upon as a new incarnation of one of the Hindu gods and was quite pestered with the sick of all diseases waiting to be cured".

In 1841, when their first child Eliza was seven and Sheppard John was five, the family left Monghyr to journey to Britain for a holiday, the main reason being to allow Andrew to recover from the effects of jungle fever which he had contracted in 1837 during his travels in India. Before leaving, Andrew preached a farewell sermon, the text of which still survives. They travelled north to Scotland but Andrew was disappointed to find that old friends had died and others didn't recognise him. They returned to India in 1843, Andrew wishing to return to his missionary work, but later decided to stay in Calcutta as the pastor of the Circular Road Baptist Church.

"I will not conceal from you that my predilections are in favour of a Missionary life in the interior, but should it appear that God has work for me to do in Calcutta, I hope I shall not run counter to his will."

He stayed in Calcutta and continued to suffer from the effects of the jungle fever until his death in 1870, having been pastor for 22 years. Six soldiers from the Regiment at Dum Dum carried him to his grave in the Dissenter's Burial Ground. A tablet in the Circular Road Church commemorates him, a few feet away from his father-in-law, John Chamberlain. Andrew Leslie's wife, Mary Ann, survived him and lived until 1891.

Sheppard John married Mary Burgh Lish and had seven children, my grandfather Franklin Marston Leslie being the sixth child. Franklin married Emma Helen Addis, between them having five children, my mother Marjorie being the fourth child, all of whom were born in India.

As far as is known, Sheppard never left India after a childhood holiday to Great Britain with his parents in 1841-2. When he died at the age of sixty-three, he was buried at Barrackpore.

GODLIEB VAN SOMEREN

Of the Dutch side of the family, a distant relative, Godlieb van Someren was yet another missionary. One of his forefathers was Governor of Dutch India, and he himself was a member of the British East India Company. He lived in Madras as a wholesaler and built himself a fine, airy house there.

The East India Company received a royal charter on New Year's Eve 1600 from Queen Elizabeth of England to be the sole trader in India. This was later renewed. In the course of time it acquired large estates, and in 1758 bought in the extensive kingdom of the Grand Mogul in the north. Tough, purposeful, surviving the worst of difficulties, the company cast its net across the entire peninsula, as far as the snowy Himalayan uplands. It laid the foundations for the subsequent Indo-British Empire. It actually did not lag far behind the heathen and Mohammedan rulers in cruelty, betrayal and greed. From the start it was antagonistic towards missions. When, in 1793 in the English parliament, there was a call for missionaries *"who might gradually bring about the spread of wholesome knowledge and raise the moral and religious condition of the Indian people"*, the company's representatives declared bitterly:-

"Sending out missionaries is the stupidest zealots' project that has ever been proposed. Such a plan militates against all reason and political health, and will endanger the peace and safety of our possessions".

Godlieb van Someren, caught up in the religious revival in England at the turn of the century (1800) was, with his decidedly Christian position, an exception among the members of the Company. It is possible that he experienced some enmity among the members of the Company because of his beliefs. If a sailing ship came in sight in those days, he was in the habit of enquiring if there were clergy or missionaries on board. These he would invite to his house. Most of them brought letters of recommendation to him. In the diary of Mary Crisp (nee van Someren 1828 in Madras) she wrote:

"Our house was always open to Christian guests, and few ministers or missionaries landed at Madras without bringing a letter of introduction to my father, who had great and heartfelt sympathy for all missionary work".

One of these missionaries relates how, arriving in Madras one Sunday morning, the hot sun already beating down, he was brought by boat from the ship, through the dangerous surf. He was taken in a palanquin through the tumult of the native town to Godlieb's house to the north, where the Europeans lived. Godlieb, just on his way out of church, received him kindly. Missionaries of the various societies, chaplains of the military presence maintained by the Company and clergy for the English community all found a gathering place in his house and, as was sometimes needful, help in both word and deed.

A friend wrote (in English) in these emotional terms upon his departure:

"Many are the years that have rolled away since we first mingled our songs of prayer upon the domestic altar and in the public temple, and pleasant have been the joys and sweet the intercourse of our kindred spirits. May they be only types of those pure and perfect pleasures which shall be found in the portion of our cup in the mansions of the blessed, or in the golden streets of the new Jerusalem. There are no friends in India from whom I shall part with greater regret than you and your beloved partner; nor are there any in the western or eastern world for whose best interests in time and eternity my heart will more warmly beat. May God eminently bless both you and yours evermore, so devoutly and fervently prays

Your affectionate friend

H. Reeve,

Madras, Jan 28th 1834"

Another wrote: (also in English)

"Our knowledge of each other is a link in providence, connected with so many others that a long chain in eternity will appear to have depended upon it. Their friendship will be refined and perpetuated by ties over which death can have no power. Oh! Should ours prove means by which any channel has been opened for the honour of the Redeemer, we shall, indeed, review it as a bright spot in this world's existence, and will strike a bright anthem to its commemoration. This is the anxious wish of one who will ever prove in all the reality of the term a sincere and affectionate friend.

R. Eives"

When Missionary Cordes, the pioneer of the Leipzig Mission, came out, and was still undecided whether or not to bend his steps towards Tranquebar in the small Danish colony, Godlieb advised him openly not to become part of the work of the old German missionaries there. This was because he believed, rightly or wrongly, that the Halle/Danish Mission (with Ziegenbaig, Schwartz, Fabricius and others), and likewise later the Leipzig one, had, by their recognition of the cast system, made a compromise with Hinduism and a concession to heathen practice. He therefore suggested to him that he begin a new work, as seemed right from his point of view. These were the problematical times when evangelical missions were in their infancy, and they lasted well into the middle of the last century. Clear light needed first to be shed on the many difficult questions, both within and without, regarding heathendom, and indeed, regarding relations between the missionaries themselves. Godlieb followed the development and outcomes of missions in various locations with lively interest and with quiet sympathy. The dark night of heathendom, that heavy burden upon the Indian people, stood constantly before his eyes. *When would the curtain be drawn aside? When would light penetrate the darkness? Would a day come when the Gospel message, bringing freedom and peace to these fettered souls, was carried to all places?* These questions must often have exercised him.

Averse to all forms of pretence, Godlieb also laid little value on the outward advantages of birth and riches. Arthur van Someren, one of his grandsons, wrote:

"When my grandfather Godlieb van Someren was in his prime, he called my father (his eldest son William) and his son Charles to him and, telling them that he had come to the conclusion that worldly position and its wealth was harmful to those professing Christianity, he, in their presence, burned the old vellum Patents of our Nobility of centuries standing and renounced all right, claim and title to the Estates and Nobles rank".

The sole son from his second marriage, Godlieb, went to Holland after his father was long dead in order to reinstate the family rights. But since he was a younger son, and since the destruction of the papers had not taken place in his presence, but in the presence of his eldest brother William, the sole heir to the title and the properties in Holland; and since also the latter, out of piety towards his father and because of his own similar convictions, was not prepared to realise his rights, these efforts were in vain. So likewise were the attempts from England in recent times to negotiate the recovery of the large ancestral estate, which has now been under Dutch rule for over 100 years, after the rights to it had long since lapsed. The sole survivor of the two witnesses, William, has now also died.

The van Someren coat of arms is still to be seen on many objects still in existence; *'Three golden sheaves on a sable shield, chevron or'*, the full coat of arms showing a rising sun over rolling waves in white and red, below which is the motto '*Dies veniet*' meaning '*The day will come!*' Our forefathers expected and looked for the day when their lineage would again attain its one-time power and importance.

Thus it was that Godlieb embodied the belief that outward honour and riches were harmful and a hindrance to the inner life of a Christian. The step he took was of great consequence to his family as he was opposed in principle, and also renounced, the old aristocratic title and property not simply for himself as his father's eldest son but also, by so doing, took away the right to it from his own eldest son and from his descendants. His children now had to remake their lives, diligently and faithfully, without any particular inherited advantages.

Opportunities for missionary work now offered themselves in especial measure, so that from then until the present time it has gone on continuously in one part of the family. Although inclined to the Baptist teaching, Godlieb embraced the totality of God's Kingdom and its missionary. That his life was not without influence upon the natives was shown by their great numbers attending his funeral, where a long procession of heathen and Muslims accompanied him to his last resting place.

FOOD FOR THOUGHT (Cont'd)

On looking back, I cannot remember ever feeling *comfortable* in church, other than when completely alone to soak up the atmospheric vibrations of an old historic building and the energy around me; I could never really come to terms with its being the 'house of God', and that to speak loudly was not the 'done thing', a high degree of reverence being called for. I was christened, attended Sunday School, and later confirmed as were most of my peers. It was not deemed fit for Christian children to be left without these accoutrements for a good and stable life, and those who managed to avoid it were not really thought of very highly, their parents being viewed as rather irresponsible. Sundays were reserved for everything 'holy', and even some of my friends were never allowed to play on that day. My own mother, however, viewed this with some disdain, thinking it quite ridiculous, thank goodness!

Of course the ultimate belief is that of believing in oneself! It is disturbing to think that so many of us give up on life when there is so much of it left to live. Statistics show that men, rather than women, have a much higher rate of suicide, not being able to see beyond, and not possessing the ability to turn that despair into hope. Men on the whole see life in a sort of 'tunnel vision', black and white, right and wrong, and have really done so since the evolution of our species where the male thought little above food and sex (hunting for food and that of procreation), his mind on one thing at a time, whereas the female's world was multi-coloured, multi-faceted in that she was able to think of several things at once, and still does! The male and female brains are wired differently in that men, obviously physically the stronger, on the whole possess technical and practical qualities, with a straightforward approach to life, whereas women link everything to emotion and are adept at dealing with the problems of bringing up children, running a household, and anything that may come their way. This inability for men to see into the future is very sad, and when the decision is made to end a life, there is very often no turning back, whereas in most cases of women 'attempting' suicide it is a cry for help, and rarely seen as final, with the innate belief that *someone* will hear, that there is a 'better' life out there, and that 'change' is possible. However, this match of physical strength in men and emotional strength in women is obviously a perfect match, and has been throughout the history of mankind!

I wonder how much of the pattern of our lives, and customs of today, we owe to the distant past – to the Druids and the worship of Pagan gods?

In conclusion, it is blatantly obvious that 'man', on the whole, is definitely in need of reassurance, a belief in a higher power in which to communicate his innermost feelings, plus hopes (and prayers) for a better quality of life on earth as well as in the 'afterlife'.

Albert Einstein:-

"The religion of the future will be a cosmic religion. It will transcend personal God and avoid dogma and theology".

"If people are good only because they fear punishment, and hope for reward, then we are a sorry lot indeed".

A SPIRITUAL STORY

I am about to recount an event which occurred many years' ago, and something that had a strange impact on my understanding of the 'supernatural' or 'spiritual'.

My husband (whom I had recently divorced) had just died – not the best of husbands, but that is not my story. However, left on my own with my children I felt desperately lonely and lost, so much so that my thoughts turned to a clairvoyant whose advertisement I had seen in the local newspaper. I hungrily sought some form of reassurance from him that my existence on this earth had a purpose, and that my life would eventually become less desolate and painful.

I telephoned him and poured out my troubles, to which he listened carefully, and implored him to help me in any way he could. I was told to find something 'blue', and if I had a cross, to hold both in my hand and go to bed. I found a silver cross of my daughter's, and the only article that was remotely blue was an ordinary leather purse of a turquoise hue that I had in my handbag!

I went to bed, by now feeling more than a little silly. I lay there staring at the ceiling and, as you can imagine, thinking it a total waste of time and that this person I had just been talking to was a little unhinged.

I lay, clutching the cross and the turquoise purse, for what seemed to be roughly ten to fifteen minutes, and was about to give up this ridiculous ritual, when I was no longer 'there'. I was surrounded by a dazzling white light that merged to gold round the edges – my whole body 'glowed', and a feeling of such joy and peace enveloped me that to try to explain it in words would be impossible. I can only say that the feeling I had was quite outside and beyond any 'earthly' emotion ever experienced before or perhaps could ever be experienced again. Whilst I floated on this incredible cloud of euphoria, high above my own body, I could look down and see myself as though totally detached from anything terrestrial. I remember saying out loud *"Please* don't make me leave" over and over again. How long this feeling lasted is impossible to tell as there seemed to be no semblance of time, but leave I had to, and I emerged feeling as though I had just been given a brief glimpse of another world, to which I *knew* I belonged.

There is so much more we have yet to learn about ourselves in the form of the 'spiritual' side of our makeup; energy most of us have not thought to tap into, and for some of us, even believed in. I am fairly certain this will be part of our lives in the future, when we have learnt to rise above the material.

Who are we to say there is nothing 'beyond'? In *my* mind I now know where I am going.

In delving into the origins of Christianity, the truth behind the story of the birth of Jesus and his Crucifixion, and the beliefs around the world, I have tried to give 'food for thought', and to bring to attention the fact that 'the facts' are perhaps not as accurate as we have been led to believe. My intention has never been to disparage anyone's belief in a 'higher power', only to shed light on a subject that will inevitably, in the future, be more freely open to discussion and dissection.

"If people are good only because they fear punishment and hope for reward, then we are a sorry lot indeed".

Phillippa Leslie

Made in the USA
Columbia, SC
03 August 2017